"Rachel's book is a call... peace and order aren't just for bishops, priests, ... offers the same calmness and clarity to all of us — even those who live in a busy world with lots to juggle."
— BISHOP ROBERT REED, president,
The CatholicTV Network

"Rachel Balducci's *Make My Life Simple* is a must-read for a busy mother caught in the whirlwind of keeping her home, her career, her family, and her sanity together. For those of us whose pendulum swings from zenning out in the art of laundry perfection to foraging the bottom of our freezer for chocolate chips during Lent, this book is a perfect reminder that order in our chaos can come from something as small as a clean kitchen sink or an improvised family prayer of gratitude. This spiritual and practical refresher is like the 30-minute workout that can get us back on track when everything seems to be spinning out of control in our secret quest for perfection. As a fellow member of the 'black Sharpie to-do list club,' I feel intense appreciation for Rachel's insight into the simplicity behind the solutions to the complex equations of life."
— JEANNIE GAFFIGAN, writer, producer, mother of five

"Benedictine monks have known for 1,500 years that an ordered *habitus* (home) is necessary to building the spiritual disciplines that, over time, order our souls to God's will. Rachel Balducci brings this practical ancient wisdom to bear on daily Christian living. You don't have to be a mystic to make your bed every morning, or a doctor of the Church to do the dishes each night. But as Rachel shows, being faithful in these small habits in your family's domestic monastery lays the groundwork for a life of conversion and abundance."
— ROD DREHER, author of *The Benedict Option*

"This is not just another book about how to organize your life. There is plenty of practical help in these pages, but more importantly, Rachel encourages us to consider all the work we do as women, all those things that stress us out and threaten our peace, and to bring order to them in light of our relationship

with God. Invite God in! Take a breath! Look at the bigger picture! It's not easy, but it is simple, and this simple book is a gift of encouragement for any woman drowning in chaos."
— DANIELLE BEAN, manager at CatholicMom.com

"Feeling like you're drowning? Does life seem anything but simple? Rachel Balducci is a loving sister guiding you above water. In *Make My Life Simple*, she will coach you into letting God's merciful, ordering hand heal that overwhelming, sinking feeling that has you trapped in the grip of anxiety and fear. *Do not be afraid! It's not all up to you.* Have faith and hope and you will be freed to love more fully, be present to the people in your life, and joyfully live God's unique plan for you, his beloved."
— KATHRYN JEAN LOPEZ, senior fellow, National Review Institute, and editor-at-large, *National Review*

"Peace. Simplicity. Let's be honest, these words escape most of us who are in the trenches of raising babies, but coming to our aid is another mama who has been there and done that. Rachel Balducci provides easy, practical, and spiritual ways to simplify our lives so that we can better enjoy those tiny humans we co-created. In a time where chaos and busyness threaten motherhood, *Make My Life Simple: Bringing Peace to Heart and Home* offers a balanced approach for women and their families. This book should be on every new mama's baby registry!"
— LEAH DARROW, speaker and author of *The Other Side of Beauty* and *Decent Exposure*

"I'm greedy for more mentors in my life. So, the chance to have Rachel Balducci — mom to FIVE boys and a daughter — spill all her lessons from the last couple decades of parenting is the most delicious gift. Practical and generous, this is, I'm pretty sure, the next best thing to getting to sit down and pick her brain in person."
— LISA-JO BAKER, best-selling author of *Never Unfriended* and *Surprised by Motherhood*

# make my life *simple*

○⊂⊃○

## bringing peace to
## heart and home

# RACHEL BALDUCCI

**Our Sunday Visitor**

www.osv.com
Our Sunday Visitor Publishing Division
Our Sunday Visitor, Inc.
Huntington, Indiana 46750

For Isabel,
who came along when I couldn't possibly handle
one more thing in life.

I'm so glad God knew better.

# table of contents

# first things first

When I first considered a book on order, inspired by a life of order, I was a mom with six kids at home. I had recently started working outside the home after spending eighteen years making work fit within my at-home schedule. Like mothers everywhere, I've always seen motherhood as my primary vocation, but personally had decided that my professional life needed to fit within my home life. I had found a way to balance a career as a writer and speaker with being a wife and mother, a schedule that worked for me as someone married to a busy attorney who owned his own practice. Add to this the fact that by our sixth anniversary, Paul and I had four sons. Early on, me staying home made the most sense.

But the years went on, and we added another son and (hooray!) a daughter at the end. Five boys and one sweet little girl. Life was busy and crazy and fun. During those years, I wrote from home and traveled for speaking engagements, and this compartmentalization worked well. I could go away for a few days for work and leave highly specific lists in extra-large black Sharpie font, and it was business as usual for my husband and kids until I returned.

When our daughter, Isabel, started kindergarten, I worried that I would feel bored. After so many years of being home and fitting work in between juggling small children, the thought of an entire day with no kids at home seemed vast and empty. It was probably time to find something to do to fill those hours. "What kind of a stay-at-home mom doesn't have kids at home with her?" I asked, rhetorically.

This was the question I posed to myself, and I should have sat still long enough to consider the answer. Indeed, what kind of stay-at-home mom doesn't have kids at home during the day? The answer is, plenty. Moms of bigger kids know what I had not yet learned: just because your children are at school for a few hours does not mean you will feel sad, lonely, and bored. Bored?! Perish the thought. Not to worry, boredom doesn't seem to be on the horizon anytime soon.

But I did not wait for an answer to my question, and I didn't stop to think through all the ways my already full schedule wouldn't clear out only because my youngest was now in kindergarten.

So I signed up to teach full-time at the school my children attend.

And it was wonderful. I absolutely loved it. I loved connecting with the students; I loved learning as much as I taught; I loved being out and away from my home, and generally all the joy and excitement of a new adventure. I loved the change of scenery, and I loved meeting a need. Our small, private school needed an English teacher, and I was able to help. It was new and exciting, and I was exactly where I was supposed to be.

Around this time, I started to think about how being organized brings peace — the problem was, I didn't understand yet what peace means. When you have a nice system for the many moving parts of your life, I decided, you can do anything. If you have a smart, efficient method for keeping the house clean, making a menu and paying your bills, then you are allowed to move about the calendar as freely as you please.

But this is not realistic, and I'm so glad a book didn't get written by me in that stage. You can indeed do anything when you have a few free hours on your daily calendar, but the fruit of doing *all the things all the time* is not good. I learned this the hard way.

Fast forward a few years. I had been teaching at the school for three years, and in the meantime we sent our oldest son off to college and watched our second son graduate from high school. The next year we would have our third high school graduation in four years, with a one-year break before yet another son's graduation. When you have your first four children in five years, those children finish high school at a shocking rate.

Life was moving at a dizzying speed, and my brain and heart were beginning to wrestle with this new season. We were no longer a family all under one roof. I was no longer dropping off all my sweet little babies at the same school, all of us riding in the same giant van. We were dispersed, slowly moving from a life that was like a solid block of cheese to a life that had been set on the counter too long and was spreading out, melting.

In my brain, that's how things felt. All the things I needed to keep track of were no longer in one solid chunk. Gone were the days of multiple boys on the same sports teams, of all my children coming and going from the same K–12 school. Now, we were all over the place. My people were no longer simply in my home or at school, but moving away, going to college, and coming and going at all hours of the day and night.

The "little things mean a lot" approach to organization worked when my kids were little. Make your lunches the night before, put people in bed before they are overtired, have a calendar that lays out the week. However, as my children grew and our world expanded, I knew that those little things were great, but inner peace had to come from a much deeper well. Suddenly, the day didn't end at 8:30 p.m., or even by 10:00! Bigger kids stay up late to study for exams; they come and go at different hours. My brain was going, going, going because I thought my fabulous organizational skills meant I could do every single thing I wanted to do. Suddenly, those methods that I thought were the key to doing it all (planning ahead and sticking to the plan) were no longer effective. They helped, but they didn't stop the tiny hamster that was running inside my head.

And so I began to question my approach to order and peace. I realized that God is indeed an ocean of peace, and that he wants that peace for each one of us. But how we will find that peace will shift and expand within the different seasons of our life. Now that my world is a little more complicated, the peace I need will come from sources other than a clean front room and the joy of a well-oiled laundry system. (Also, nap time no longer exists. Just saying.)

What do I mean when I talk about peace? Peace is considered to be the presence of harmony and the absence of conflict. So when we talk about peace within ourselves, we mean the presence of harmony in our thoughts and attitudes, in our home and in our relationships. Peace means a lack of conflict in our soul, in our relationships with God and with those around us.

Despite my best efforts to get on top of my angst and anxiety, I was overwhelmed to the core. No amount of list-making and prior planning quelled the weird feelings in my gut. I felt nervous all the time. I was always going over what I needed to do next, where we needed to go next, how we were going to get all the things done for everyone: for my kids, for my students, for the many sub-groupings on my daily calendar (Carline! Staff meeting! Doctors' appointments! Writing deadlines!)

What had started as a wonderful, peaceful commitment to work at my children's school had become my driving focus. No one had done that to me except myself — me and my desire to say yes and be involved and help out with everything. And so, about six weeks into that school year, I looked up and realized that I was on complete overload.

So many things in my personal life had changed in such a short amount of time. Because of that, what had worked for us as a family a few years before was now causing strife for me, which meant strife for my family. Because I had committed to so much, my outside-the-home obligations took my best energy, and I gave to my kids what was left. My children, my sweet babies, were one more entry on my never-ending Today's To-Do List. Sure, I was organized, but I was also a complete mess.

I was talking this over one day with a trusted friend, who added, "Yes! And your husband!" And it was then I realized I hadn't even added Paul to the list of "stuff I'm giving my time and energy to." Meeting up for lunch no longer happened, and date nights had become obsolete. Once upon a time, we put our children to bed at 7 p.m. and enjoyed the rest of the evening together. Now our teenagers stayed up later than us, or I went to bed after putting our younger children to bed and let Paul stay up with our big guys.

Things had gotten horribly out of balance. Good organization is not a substitute for true order. My life was out of order, and it was costing me.

I remember standing in my dad's classroom. (Yes! We taught together in classrooms across the hall from each other, and it was the best! You can see why I loved being at the school.) "I feel like I am able to perfectly manage this," I told my dad, holding up my hands about the size of an eight-pound bass, "but I can barely function when the day looks like this," and I moved my hands out to what you would make that fish if you were bragging. If anything extra was added to my day (and it always did get added), smoke streamed out of my ears.

"You don't have a margin," my dad gently pointed out. In the midst of our conversation, he could tell that I was operating much too close to the limits of what I could peacefully handle. That meant that regular life was at the outer edge of peace, with no room for taking a breath.

He was right.

And so, I sent an email to my boss saying I had to cut back. I thought I could limp along until the end of the school year. But it was only November, which wasn't a good sign.

Truthfully, I had to make changes immediately. I was beginning to look at my life as one giant never-ending to-do list. There was no joy. There was no peace. Heck, I never even noticed the weather anymore. Was it cold? Was it hot? I didn't know. I ran from my van to drive somewhere to get out, go in and do something, and get back in the van. I was sad and conflicted because I loved working at the school. But I knew, deep down, that my life was disordered.

I had become such a bundle of anxiety and exhaustion that I needed a complete reset. My family needed me. They needed me physically present, to help with all the things a mother does. But they needed me emotionally present, spiritually present, which meant not being someone who stared down every day, wishing it was already over.

God didn't want me to live that way, running around like a chicken with my head cut off. He doesn't want that for any of us. He wants us to have joy and freedom. And yes, he needs our "Yes!" to do the things he's asked of us, but we need to carefully and mindfully consider what those actually are. We all have commitments, things we have to say yes to. We have loved ones, obligations, and responsibilities. We aren't free to cut all the cords and walk away.

But we can have order, and we can have peace.

At some point in the midst of those weeks of slowly, ever so slowly admitting to myself that my life, my being, was in a state of disorder, I called my mama. In tears, I admitted to her that I felt sad and exhausted, and I was also starting to have panic attacks driving down the highway (I'm nothing if not dramatic).

"You know you can quit, Rach," she said. And instantly, I remember it so clearly, it was like she had rotated the valve of my emotional pressure cooker. All the pent-up fear and anxiety I had been holding on to was released, because for the first time I realized there might be a solution, that I didn't need to keep living this way. That life could be wonderful and joyful again, if I could find the ability to take control of — and simplify — the pace.

I was so grateful that she said those words, even if I had no intention of following her advice. "Of course I can't quit," I thought. "Everyone needs me and all the gifts I have to offer! I bring so much to the table, how can they get along without me?" It's possible a little pride was mixed into the equation.

One night, as I was crying out to God in the midst of my stress, I heard him tell me something. It was one of those moments when you know it's God because you wouldn't, you couldn't, come up with these words in this moment of your life.

"Saying yes to me," I heard him say, "doesn't mean saying yes to everything!"

And that, my friend, was the light-bulb moment of the century.

Teaching at the school was a good thing. But I had allowed my sense of mission and purpose — my sense of talents and abilities — to be shifted from my primary responsibility to my husband and children toward my job outside the home. Things were out of balance because what was required of me to continue this kind of life-outside-the-home pace was more than I had to give.

A few weeks later, I walked away from the job altogether.

Saying no is a difficult decision. Saying yes makes people so much happier. Not that people make you feel bad for saying you can't do something. It's a lot more fun when you can give them an answer that is going to make their life easier: "Yes! I will cover that need. Yes! I can help you out with this."

But I was on burnout, and I had to change.

It was embarrassing and difficult for me to walk away from my job. Honestly, I felt like a failure. The only reason I could call my boss and say I needed to stop working was an emergency my husband had at his law practice. He was in a season of needing me to be present to him as he worked through big issues, and that gave me the courage to step away from teaching. Thank you, Lord, for kind and loving people who gave me the freedom to utter those words, "I can't keep doing this."

And so, I came back home. I began to put my main energy and focus back into my family. And within a few months, I started to craft order, which brought me peace.

## order brings peace

Now, this is not a book about how leaving your job and staying at home will solve all your problems. The world is filled with working moms, and I am grateful for that. We need women in the workforce, bringing their light and wisdom and spirit to the world. And when that's what a woman is supposed to be doing, there is grace for it. Whether a woman works because she has to or because she wants to, when it is what is best for the family (for the money, for a woman's use of her skills and interests, for her sanity), it is a feasible option. I love that we all have the freedom to make that decision. We each need to prayerfully consider, within ourselves and with our spouse, what our family needs. And then we proceed. We are either outside the home from 9 to 5 or we aren't. Maybe we are away in the evenings, or maybe being away in the evenings is the least peaceful solution. Maybe we work nights a few days a week to be home the rest. Whatever it is, once you find the rhythm that works, you will feel it.

For me, I had achieved the biggest factor of order: I had simplified the disorder of my priorities. While quitting a job you love isn't always the answer, in this situation I knew it was. My commitments had drained my energy, and I had nothing left to give my family. My husband and children deserved a version of me that wasn't completely used up on all my other endeavors.

The first step in order is identifying your priorities and directing your energy accordingly. We proceed from there.

But first, let's talk about what it means to have order. We need to understand what true order is by first addressing what it isn't.

Order isn't a matter of having the most organizational bins or the most detailed calendar. It's not about labeled shelves and clearly marked containers. Those are all nice to have, but order is much bigger than that.

Maintaining order in our lives means keeping our priorities straight. It's having an understanding of what God has asked me to do, and then doing it. Order means giving the proper amount of attention to what truly matters. This takes a lot of work.

Think of it like this: You are trying to get out the door to take your children to the park. You have an hour to get there and back, which is great if you are ready to go right this minute. But when it's time to leave, you can't find the toddler's shoe. And then, after twelve minutes spent scouring the house, you realize you also don't have your car keys. By the time you have rounded up all the things you need to get out the door and have an adventure, half your time is gone.

We can all relate to that concept of order; this is order at its most practical (and where the idea of clearly labeled bins and containers makes sense). But expand this concept to a larger scale. Our "keys" and "shoes" are things that take away our time. Maybe it's spending too much time on the internet; maybe it's investing too many hours outside of your primary vocation. It might be spending too much time feeling tired or angry or sad.

If we haven't taken care of the basics, day-to-day living is crazy. When we're busy with all the small things, what we need to be doing (the good stuff) gets less of our attention.

So when we talk about order, we mean having all the events in our life taking up the proper amount of our time and energy. Searching for our keys isn't what life is all about, but for too many of us, the scramble of the nitty gritty leaves us feeling worn out before we even start the things we actually want and need to be doing.

Order in life means understanding, appreciating, and recognizing the season of life I'm in, and then proceeding accordingly.

For example, a mother with small children should not put pressure on herself to have a prayer life that looks like a nun living in a cloister. God has given her the vocation of motherhood, and she is in a unique season of having small children. Those two things (motherhood, small children) take priority over what she might consider an "ideal" prayer life. The ideal is actually doing what God has asked of her right now (being a mom to small children!) and letting everything else in her life work around that.

That is true order and simplicity: recognizing my vocation, and where I am in regards to that, and allowing every other detail to fall into place around it.

From this comes peace.

Peace isn't only about feeling good about the stuff I'm doing, or following my passions (though your passions are important). Peace comes from acknowledging that Jesus has a specific purpose for my life and that he will give me the grace, wisdom, and time to get it all done. Peace comes from always asking God to be in the center of what I'm doing, and asking God if what I'm doing is what he wants me to do.

The thing about order is that it happens on a very large scale. Maybe it's even on a variety of scales. First off, we must have the big picture in order — am I doing what I need to be doing? Is my time and energy being used in ways that serve me and my family? Are we making the money we need? Are the practical and emotional needs of each family member being met? The beautiful part of family life is that each individual family must find the answers to those questions, to be honest within the family unit, and then do what works best. We consider all the factors and find the work/life balance that we need.

From there, we work for order in our home, order in a practical sense.

And we work for order within our person, order in our body, mind, and spirit.

And finally, we need order in our relationship with God, which impacts the way we see ourselves and the way we interact with the world around us.

That is a lot of order to maintain! If we think too much about it, we can get overwhelmed.

The best way to maintain a sense of order is not to think too much about the bigger picture on a minute-by-minute basis, but to focus on simplifying the small aspects of our lives that come together to bring us peace. Even our order needs to be in the right order! When we find the right balance, slowly we move in the direction of a peaceful existence. Instead of moving through our days, putting out fires or simply surviving, we are able to thrive.

"Most people don't do their maintenance and end up controlled by emergencies," says Christian author and speaker Joyce Meyer. Isn't that the truth! When we are running so ragged that we don't have time to get ahead of anything, our day is dictated by the next urgent deadline. Meyer relayed a story of only going to the dentist when she had a major toothache. By avoiding regular cleanings (because she was afraid of going), she was always dealing with urgent situations. Because she didn't take care of matters proactively, she was controlled by the worst-case scenario.

Here is the benefit of true order and peace: when we are paying attention to the little things, with the right amount of energy and focus, we can eliminate that rat-race feeling. Yes, emergencies will arise. But those will be the exception rather than the rule.

Order and simplicity aren't the equivalent of perfection. In fact, a great deal of peace comes from letting go of a desire to be perfect. We don't show the world we are Christians by our perfection — but we have a peace that cannot be bought or faked.

Order brings peace. Order doesn't bring a life free of mistakes or a guarantee that we won't ever suffer or feel tired or overwhelmed. But order can help us cut out the fat, help us operate within boundaries and margins that protect us from losing our way.

Lives can have order in so many ways. We can have order in our home, in our thinking, in the way we relate to other people. We need order in our prayer life, and order in our approach to our attitudes about time, money, and talent. There are so many details that make up a day, and when we spend

enough time tweaking them (not too much, not too little)
we begin to find the simplicity we need to fill our days with
peace. Simplicity and peace come from a life of order, which
means each task gets the energy and attention it needs.

## comparison is the thief of peace

Order and peace and organization and limits — all these
things will look different for different people. That was part of
my challenge in my journey toward redirecting and reviving
my focus. I looked at the women around me, who seemed to
be doing the exact same thing as me and then some. I was
especially aware of the women who worked at the school full-
time alongside me, who also had children still at home and
seemed to manage it all beautifully. They spent more hours
at the school than I did and didn't seem the least bit frazzled.

Unfortunately, I allowed that comparison to make me
blind to my own struggle. If they can do it, I reasoned, I should
be able to!

In his book on restoring sanity to overloaded lives, Dr.
Richard Swenson is quick to point out that physical and mental stress looks different for different people.

"Individuals differ significantly regarding how much stress
is desirable or what types of events are distressing," he writes
in *Margin*. "What strains some does not bother others.... A
stressor that for one might be pleasure, for another might be
pain. For one, the price of life; for another, the kiss of death."

People have different levels of stress that they can tolerate,
as well as different events that cause stress in different ways. So
one event that I might find totally relaxing, you might find
completely stressful. And vice versa.

"We must understand," Dr. Swenson writes, "that everyone has a different tolerance for overload and a different
threshold level when breakdown begins to occur. It is important for us to set people free to seek their own level."

In other words, don't compare!

True peace and order, a simplified life, has at its core a true understanding of what God is asking of *you*. This is why it's so important to always be working toward closer union with God — we have to have a real relationship with him to understand what it is he wants of us. It's not enough to look at the people around you, people with similar gifts or at a similar place in life. In fact, this could lead to envy and absolute burnout! While it's nice to be inspired by those around us, we do have to keep our eyes on our own paper.

Here is where a holistic approach to simplicity and peace comes in. We pay attention to our spiritual, mental, and physical needs, and we make lots of small efforts to care for the many areas of our life. We make decisions based on prayer and common sense, and not by looking to see what other people are up to. So much peace and freedom come when we learn to be who we are, who God made each of us to be, and to live the life he called each one of us to live. Personally, I'm the wife and mom of the Family Balducci, and there is no other family out there exactly like us! Paul and I will make decisions for our family life with criteria that won't look like anyone else's.

It's so much easier to do the right thing for yourself and for your family when you aren't trying to keep up with those around you.

## set healthy limits

Know yourself, be honest with yourself. We have to be willing to recognize our stressors, our limits, and not worry when that looks different from those around us. We must allow others to be at peace with their own limitations as well. Problems arise when we find those limits and ignore them.

"Some," Dr. Swenson writes, "will respond, 'I can do all things through Christ who strengthens me.' Does this mean you can fly? Can you go six months without eating? Neither can you live a healthy life chronically overloaded. God did not intend this verse to represent a negation of life-balance."

If we want peace, we have to be willing to admit we have limits.

"Not all threshold limits are appreciated as we near them," says Dr. Swenson, "and it is only in exceeding them that we suddenly feel the breakdown." You don't know you're on overload until you've overloaded.

What I've learned in this journey is that we can have order on many levels, but we need to be taking all these aspects into consideration together. Our body, mind, and spirit each know when things are out of order. If you are drinking too much caffeine, your body will tell you. If your focus is always negative, your mind will suffer. And when you run yourself ragged, even if there are enough hours in the day, your spirit will eventually send up a flare and beg you to reconsider.

It's okay to admit you are on overload. God didn't create us to do all the things all the time. In fact, built right into our first glimpse of God in Genesis, he creates a day for us to rest. He wants us to take time to reboot, to catch our breath, and to look at the beauty around us instead of going, going, going.

Time off, observing the Sabbath, slowing down at the end of the day — these take effort. We must fight for quiet, especially in a world that makes twenty-four hours of productivity a possibility (have you ever checked your email in the middle of the night? It's possible to never step away from the To-Do's!).

We have to work for margins of sanity. We need to fight to maintain that healthy space that exists between doing what we need to do and the state of absolute burnout.

"He restores my soul," says Psalm 23:3. Part of the way God restores us is by enabling us with common sense that uses our body, mind, and spirit to guide us away from doing too much. The body can handle a lot of stress, but when it gets past the point of healthy stress, it will tell you. Remember those panic attacks I had while driving down the highway? That was my body trying to tell me to step back.

If you are living with that concrete-block-on-my-chest

feeling all the time, your body might be trying to tell you to adjust something.

When we start finding that life feels exhausting or that we are always sad or angry or sick, it's time to consider all the things we have going on and figure out what needs to change.

That's called *limits*, my friend, and they are there to keep us sane.

## God cares

In the midst of all the effort to have order, peace, and a simple life filled with joy — God is there!

These efforts to streamline are efforts to hear God. When we cut away all the fat, the excess, the busy work, and the things that drag us down, it is easier to tune in to the voice of God.

The beautiful reality is that God cares about all of this, because this approach to simplicity will draw us closer to him. There is no detail too small for his gaze. God wants us to be happy, and he wants us to have the freedom to use the gifts he's given us to build the Church. Whatever that means for you in your life, God wants to help you figure that out. And when we have the right kind of order, we find the peace we need. We can hear God guiding us with his wisdom and love. This helps us move throughout our days in the life he's called each one of us to live, in a way that glorifies him.

"He is not the God of disorder but of peace," says 1 Corinthians 14:33. God cares for us and wants our lives filled with peace.

Ultimately, an ordered relationship with our Creator is at the heart of pure freedom and joy. We must know how much God loves us, and learn to experience that love. When our relationship with God is working as it should, we find the most important kind of peace — that which is deep within, abiding and transforming.

At the heart of all of our struggle for order, God is waiting. When we talk about menus, laundry, and carpool schedules,

God is tied into it. It's crazy, because too often we convince ourselves that God doesn't care about the minutiae of our day. God can't drive my carpool for me, so why should I include him in any of it?

But I have learned from experience that while God and Jesus and the Holy Spirit aren't necessarily who I consult before I plan my weekly meals, they are strangely involved in every aspect of my day. Before I do something as simple as rearrange my front room furniture, I ask for guidance from the Holy Spirit. I know that sounds weird, but when I do, he always shows up. I end up with some idea, some plan, that I never saw coming — something that is the answer to my hopes for creating a comfy space for my family to gather.

God cares.

So, yes, a prayer life and interior peace and not being overloaded with life in general — these are all important in the quest for a simplified, ordered life.

But first, let's talk about having a clean kitchen sink. Because that helps a lot too.

part I

# practical peace, order within the home

*Paperwork, cleaning the house, dealing with the innumerable visitors who come all through the day, answering the phone, keeping patience and acting intelligently, which is to find some meaning in all that happens — these things, too, are the works of peace.*
— Dorothy Day, *The Catholic Worker* (December 1965)

A n ordered life is one that gives each task the attention it deserves. This means that small tasks should get a small amount of our attention. When our lives feel out of order, we start to have an imbalance in where we put our energy. I have felt firsthand the stress that comes from the details of life being out of balance. Knowing what to cook for dinner shouldn't be some epic achievement. But when you are running around like a crazy woman, it sometimes is.

Before we proceed, I want to stress something. In family life, it's important to recognize that we go through seasons.

"Season" is one of my favorite words. I use it a lot because I think it keeps so much in perspective. The mother with a newborn baby should not be striving for the kind of order that a mom of bigger kids might have. Mamas with newborns shouldn't focus on anything other than survival. You give yourself time — six weeks, ten weeks, seven months — whatever it takes, until you start to feel some semblance of sanity and normalcy. And then, when you can peacefully begin to think "bigger picture" (beyond getting through this feeding session, the one that will end just in time for the next one to begin), it's time to come up with a plan.

This concept of "season" can apply to all kinds of times. Christmas season. Basketball season. Flu season. The weeks of your oldest child starting school outside the home. These are all times of different kinds of stress, and it's okay to say, in those seasons, that you are putting one foot in front of the other. Having four children playing on three separate teams might not be the time to be organizing all the closets. This is the time to get your children to the next practice and the next games.

But in the calmer moments, or your version of that, getting things in order, taking the time to get streamlined and to have a plan — this is what will help in the fast pace of family life. The abundant life! Isn't life wonderful. Let's proceed without feeling like we are always on the brink of drowning.

Practical peace is a focus on organization of our home and of our time. It takes effort and patience, but when we are willing to be honest with the state of things, and be willing to make changes, we will find the peace we crave. This isn't about making a home that is perfect or a schedule that is foolproof, but about making an effort to cut out enough detritus so peace can reign. An organized schedule and an organized home will clear the clutter from our mind and spirit and help us better hear what God is saying to us, what he is asking of us.

Organization is part of having peace ahead of time. It's like money in the bank or a pedicure before you realize you need to wear sandals.

But it doesn't magically appear.

"Turn from evil and do good," says 1 Peter 3:11, and "seek peace and follow after it."

If we want peace, we have to pursue it. We can't sit back and wait for life to feel peaceful. We must "turn from evil and do good."

Now I'm not saying your disorganized coat closet is evil. But it's not going to organize itself. We have to work hard to get peace and order, and it's totally worth it.

If you want to be a person of peace, you need to be willing to make the changes you need to make in order to have more peace. Make adjustments, and go after peace. Pursue peace within your home and within yourself and with your fellow man. As Joyce Meyer says: Don't just want peace; go after it.

So, what will it take to bring peace to your life? Stop for a moment and consider this. Maybe you want to make a list. What areas of your life are robbing you of your peace? Be honest with yourself. What is dragging you down? What zaps your energy and makes you want to curl up on the couch under a blanket?

Now say to yourself: "I am no longer willing to live without peace. I want peace. I will do what it takes to bring peace to my life."

What will it take? Take a moment and answer this: "How can I find the order within my home and schedule — within my brain! — that I need to find true freedom and joy?"

Let's break it down, and figure it out, and then let's go after it!

But, before that, let's get one thing straight. I'm not saying we won't have hard times. I'm not suggesting that if we get all of our ducks in the right row it's all going to be perfect. Pride tries to tell us that we won't suffer. That perfection is the answer to everything. That's not realistic. We aren't going to pursue peace by pursuing perfection.

But there is something to be said for working hard. "Pray as though everything depended on God. Work as though everything depended on you," said Saint Ignatius of Loyola. It's not enough to look at the state of your home and complain that it's a wreck. If you aren't willing to pick a few things up, I can't feel sorry for you (I'm talking to you, Rachel Balducci). God loves each one of us so very much, but he doesn't generally come into the front room to gather up the toys and wipe down the baseboards.

He does, however, give us the gifts of wisdom and smart brains. We must use those two weapons to make our lives more peaceful. It's a little bit practical, a little bit spiritual.

chapter 1

# homemaking/household management

*A true home is one of the most sacred of places....*
*Far more than we know, do the strength and beauty of our lives*
*depend upon the home in which we dwell.*

— J. R. Miller

M y friend Carrie went through a season where she was so overwhelmed in life that the only thing she could keep clean was her car. That was it. But that's what she did. She accepted the fact that for whatever reason, the house was a challenge. But if she treated the car as an extension of the house, that would be the one room she could keep clean. She kept a set of plastic drawers in the back of her minivan, and she hyper-organized those drawers, stocking them with water, snacks, first aid supplies, and anything else her family might need when they were out and about. If she couldn't accomplish what she wanted in the house, she reasoned, she would focus on the vehicle.

It's okay to not have everything perfect all of the time. In fact, that is how life is. As much as we work to find systems that get the job done and bring order to our home and spirit, we must admit right now that we are humans with human suffering. We aren't in heaven yet, and as such, things will not be perfect. It's okay. So don't think that all this advice will make everything perfect. There will always be a spot on at least one wall of the house. Some baseboard will always have a little smudge. Don't get so focused on cleanliness and order that it becomes a burden — or an idol.

But attention to homemaking and household management will make a big difference in your quest for order, for peace, for a feeling of simplified joy. It will get us moving in the right direction. And like my friend Carrie, we will start to find success and victory in the areas we know we can tackle. That's where we will find joy and peace.

# make your bed, clean the sink
*As the family goes, so goes the nation, and so goes
the whole world in which we live.*
— Pope Saint John Paul II, homily (November 30, 1986)

The very first step in finding order in life is to start with what you're staring at. What am I looking at? What is the thing right in front of my face? Let's start with that.

Each morning we get up, and staring back at us is an unmade bed. Let's make that bed!

We've all heard this so many times there's no need for me to find a source on it. The world is filled with experts who say you should start off your day making your bed. What's the big deal?

One of the best explanations I've heard is from the address given by Admiral William H. McRaven, ninth commander of U.S. Special Operations Command, at the University-wide Commencement at The University of Texas at Austin. Here's what he said:

> Every morning in basic SEAL training, my instructors,
> who at the time were all Vietnam veterans, would show

up in my barracks room and the first thing they would do was inspect my bed. If you did it right, the corners would be square, the covers pulled tight, the pillow centered just under the headboard and the extra blanket folded neatly at the foot of the rack. [That's Navy talk for bed.]

It was a simple task — mundane at best. But every morning we were required to make our bed to perfection. It seemed a little ridiculous at the time, particularly in light of the fact that we were aspiring to be real warriors, tough battle-hardened SEALs, but the wisdom of this simple act has been proven to me many times over.

If you make your bed every morning you will have accomplished the first task of the day. It will give you a small sense of pride, and it will encourage you to do another task and another and another. And by the end of the day, that one task completed will have turned into many tasks completed. Making your bed will also reinforce the fact that little things in life matter. If you can't do the little things right, you will never be able to do the big things right.

And, if by chance you have a miserable day, you will come home to a bed that is made — that you made — and a made bed gives you encouragement that tomorrow will be better.

So if you want to change the world, start off by making your bed.

Those small tasks add up to the big tasks. If you want a clean, organized house, start with a clean, organized room. If you want a clean room, start with a made bed. It's moving backward from your end goal and focusing on the first thing. And when you do that first thing first, right when you get up and get moving, the first task of the day is complete, and you are moving in the right direction.

The same can be said about the kitchen sink. When my

entire house is trashed and I'm feeling overwhelmed by it all, I generally deal with the kitchen sink first. I wash those dishes, or load them in the dishwasher. And then I wipe down that sink. I take my sponge and soap it up, and I quickly wipe down the sides, bottom, and drain of the sink. I get the section where the countertop meets the edge of the sink, scrubbing the little line that can gather grime and mildew. And then I rinse and wipe one more time. Then I have a shiny, clean, empty sink. And I work my way out from there.

Even if it takes hours for the rest of the house to get tackled, I can come back to my made bed and the clean sink and have that sense of satisfaction. This thing — this bed, this sink — is orderly. What a nice feeling!

Start small, and train your children to do the same.

The best way to teach your children the value of a clean home is to slowly begin to show them how to be a part of it. Learning to make a bed will help your children be a part of keeping the home clean, and it will also begin to ingrain in them that same sense of satisfaction and accomplishment.

## start a family blitz

*Everybody wants to save the Earth; nobody wants
to help Mom do the dishes.*

— P. J. O'Rourke, *All the Trouble in the World*

The next step in practical peace and organization is a focus on keeping one room clean. For us, the room that always get the most attention is the family room. Even if I run out of steam by the end of the night and have to leave a pile of laundry in the upstairs hallway or a bathroom in need of attention (not unusual), we always make sure the family room gets tidied.

In our family, we have something called the "twenty-minute blitz." It's simple, and it gets the job done. In addition to that, it has trained my kids to work and to understand the scope of a home-cleaning project. It's not enough to say "Go clean that room." You have to explain how to do that. And if you want your kids to be able to (eventually) tackle this on their own, you have to keep it simple.

Of our six children, the first five are boys. We had a new baby boy every twenty-one months for a while, which meant at one point we had four boys, ages five and under. Life was very crazy then and continues to be so (in all honesty). Our last baby was a girl, and now that she's in elementary school I'm blown away by how intuitive she is when it comes to knowing what I'm asking. She's not like her brothers in that regard.

In other words, if you have sons, be kind. They very rarely are able to read your mind. I'm actually grateful that I had Isabel at the end of the string of boys, because if she had been around to compare to the brothers, that would have been a struggle. I continue to be shocked and amazed by the small ways she gets what I'm saying.

With my boys, however, I learned that they need me to clearly explain what I want from them when I say, "Let's clean up." And it's important for them to learn this. At the end of every evening, instead of sending the boys to bed and leaving a messy house for mama to tackle, we would do this cleanup "blitz" together. Paul and I would divide and conquer.

Keep in mind that the best way to get this kind of job done is to have the mantra K.I.S.S. — Keep It Simple, Sister. Less is more when it comes to directing lots of little (or big) children to make family life peaceful.

Here are the steps to cleaning your home by tidying each room. Start with just one!

First, assign each member of the family a room or an area of the house. Then, within that area, be it a room or a space or even a corner, tell the person assigned to that space exactly what needs to be done. It's a little like the board game Clue! It's a person, in a room, with a specific task. "Elliott, you have the front room. I want you to straighten the throw pillows, throw away all trash that is left in there, and anything that does not belong in that room take to the room it does belong in. After that, please wipe down the coffee table and any sticky spots on the furniture."

This way, Elliott knows he's not required to vacuum (someone else does all the vacuuming), nor do I expect him to wipe the blinds or clean the TV. I've spelled it out pedantically — maybe even obnoxiously (not in tone, but in the specific nature of my directions). But in the midst of this, the job gets done to my satisfaction, and my child learns how to "clean the front room." Also, this is a win-win because your worker bees don't get frustrated when they don't live up to your expectations. There are matched expectations, and everyone walks away happy.

This method is surprisingly effective and crazy quick. We now call our blitz the Seven-Minute Blitz, because everyone knows what is required. When you streamline the work, it's a lot easier to get your kids ready to come in and get going already, because they understand (1) we work until the job is done, and (2) it doesn't take that long to get the job done.

The Family Blitz can include other approaches. Try a blitz that focuses on picking up toys — the key here is to have bins that aren't so specifically organized ("all the new-classical Star Wars figures go in this jar, red Legos in this bucket ...") that the task is a nightmare. Keep It Simple, Sister. Also use this method for wiping down a bathroom. Arm that worker with a container of cleaning wipes and send him on his way. The deep scrub can be for another time. In the Family Blitz it's about maintenance, and having a freshened sink and toilet.

# straighten the bedrooms, and the kitchen
*If you can organize your kitchen, you can organize your life.*
— Louis Parrish

I'm a big believer in helping my children keep their rooms clean. I don't mean I'm always in there cleaning up for them; but in the training stages it's important for them not only to hear that they need to clean their room but also to see how it can be done.

How do you magically get rid of clutter? You don't. You have to have a feel for what's worth keeping out on display, what's worth tucking away, and what needs to go to Catholic Social Services. Not every knickknack is for exhibition. For younger children especially (bless their little pack-rat hearts), I have had a bucket that goes either under the bed or on a bookshelf in the room, which holds all that stuff/junk/detritus/precious items that kids need to have. You can have clean and tidy bedrooms without being a cold-hearted dictator. Kids should be allowed to have their "things" — and those things don't have to take over the entire room. This will work to varying degrees depending on the child. One of my boys, if he doesn't become some kind of cloistered monk I will be shocked, because his bedroom already looks like a monk's cell. He likes a spartan bedroom and streamlines his room by letting go of extra papers, junk, and knickknacks. His brother, who is twenty-one months younger, is the exact opposite. If I'm not careful, he will leave for college with a U-Haul full of every receipt, flyer, or slip of school paper he has collected. Those kinds of children need a little more encouragement to sort through what is worth keeping.

The kitchen … I won't lie: I hate emptying the dishwasher so much that I won't let anyone else do it. That sounds weird, I know, but I dislike this task so much that the only thing worse than suffering through these four excruciating minutes is to have to watch someone else drag it out to twelve. So that's my little treat: I do it myself, when no one is under foot, and I rip it off like a Band-Aid. We all have chores like that in our homes, and I think it's perfectly acceptable and fine to decide that you will manage that one thing on your own because it's easier that way.

Of course, as mothers we have to make sure that we strike the right balance in doing things ourselves (easier, quicker, up to my standards) with having the rest of our family members help. I am greatly motivated by thinking about future daughters-in-law who will enjoy finding a man who knows how to pick up a mess.

So consider your love of sanity, and balance that out with your desire to not do all the work, divided by how much training you want to bestow.

"Good habits formed at youth make all the difference," said Aristotle. That quote is on my fridge, a reminder for me as much as for my children. We have to let them do the work, because they need to learn. Do the hard thing now: your kids (or their spouses!) will thank you for it later.

# clean your home

*My idea of housework is to sweep the room with a glance.*
— Erma Bombeck

So your house is trashed. Now what?

Life is busy. We've all had weeks where we blink and it's Friday afternoon, and the laundry hasn't been switched over since Tuesday. Even fastidious housecleaners have times like this. We can all relate to a day of cleaning that requires picking up dirty laundry from every room in the house and peeling off a popsicle stick that's been stuck to the dining room table for days. (Or is that just me?)

This can be daunting.

Cleaning your home is the precursor to keeping a home clean. So before you can implement the Family Blitz, you need to get in the habit of *cleaning your home*. However, I put the other tips first because I want you to realize that they are the end goal of this step. We clean the home to get in the habit of having a home that is clean. Once we have the starting point of clean floor, windows, and bathrooms, the daily maintenance will be much easier.

I have found that in order for the Family Blitz to be truly effective, and for my family to be a part of a clean, tidy house, I have to put in some serious sweat every seven to fourteen days. This means two to three hours of deep cleaning and picking up as you go.

I'd like to call this section "Here's What I Would Do," and then, as with all good information, I want you to take it and tweak it to work for you. You can only use a system that gets the job done in the time and manner that suit your needs.

Also, full disclosure: I've had seasons where someone came in and did my cleaning for me. Sadly, I'm one of those weirdos who never likes someone else's cleaning of my home as much as my own cleaning. But I haven't always had time to get everything done at one time, so I hire someone. I also have friends who have someone come in for an entire day and scrub the home from top to bottom. This is a dream, and if you're in a place where that works for you, I say go for it. Then you can use that nice, clean house as a starting point for your daily maintenance.

Do you remember that scene in *The Lord of the Rings: The Return of the King* when Aragorn summons the Army of the Dead? They show up with him at Minas Tirith and swarm out of the boat, a green blanket of power that destroys Sauron's entire army.

This is what you are going to do to your house.

You are going to move through your house like that army, spreading the blanket of your cleaning power, putting everything in its place, and leaving behind gleaming floors and shiny surfaces. Here's how:

1. Start with the floors and work your way up. Walk through the house and pick up everything that is on the floor. Where do these things go? Don't slow down too much to deal with tiny details, but in general get things where they need to be. Toys in the toy area, dirty clothes in the laundry room. Get dishes into the sink, and make a pile of papers. The key to getting the whole house clean in one go is that you can't allow yourself to get distracted. This won't be the time to deal with bills or paperwork or straightening a closet. Those will need to be jobs for

another time. Today, you are scrubbing.

2. Once the floors are cleared of clutter, it's time to vacuum. Start at one end of the house and work your way through. We have a two-story home, so I treat the upstairs as a separate entity from the downstairs. In general, I don't start one area before I finish the other. So vacuum your way through the house. This should be quick and easy because the floors are all cleared.

3. Next, bathrooms! Scrub the bathrooms. This is easiest when there is a pail with the cleaning supplies all ready to go. I am a huge fan of Pine-Sol for the toilets and a non-scratch cleanser for the sinks and tubs. Don't worry about the mirrors. We will come back for those later. Scrub thoroughly around the floors of the toilet, too, and try not to cry if, like me, you have five sons. This will get less emotional as they get older and develop better aim.

4. Now the floors are vacuumed, the house is picked up, and the bathrooms are cleaned. Let's mop! Get your bucket and detergent (again, Pine-Sol for me unless I'm on a Murphy's Oil Soap kick). I move through and mop; generally, about halfway through the downstairs the water looks like chocolate milk, so it's time to switch it up. Then I finish mopping, do one more bucket refresh, and carry it upstairs.

5. Next, it's time to do all of this upstairs. If I've run out of time (this happens on days when the house is particularly gross), then I will put off the upstairs for another day.

6. Quickly move through the house to clean all of the windows and mirrors with spray cleaner and microfiber clothes.

Once the house is at this starting point, it's a nice reset for the rest of the family to pitch in with the daily maintenance.

Here are a few variations on this theme:

1. Don't do all the work yourself, and don't waste a precious weekday doing it. You could do this on a Saturday and assign each family member a room to clean.
2. Do it on a Saturday, but assign each family member a task (spray clean, vacuum, mop, wipe down furniture) to get the job done.
3. Ignore it altogether and see how long anyone will notice.

I don't recommend number 3.

Before we move on, here's one last takeaway. What works for me might not work for you. You will have to decide for yourself what level of clean you need in order to have peace. Honestly, what brings me peace in terms of home cleanliness might be absolutely stressful to you. Or the reverse! Never create your home standards based on anyone else's standards. My mom, mother of eight, was able to have chore charts and clearly defined daily lists for me and each of my siblings. This has never worked for me. Maybe it's because I had those five boys in a row, but my method for getting work done around my home has always been a sneak-attack approach. "Ethan! It's your turn to take out the trash!" That method has proven to be much less stressful for me than coming up with a list of chores, assigning those chores, making the list, and following up on who is getting their work done.

The end result is the same: the work gets done, and the kids are a part of it. But my approach is one developed by me to suit my needs.

You do you, as they say. To which I will add: And there you shall find your peace.

# plan a menu
*How easy is that?*
— Ina Garten

A menu is a plan of what you and your family are going to eat for the week. "Duh," you say? Well, for years I found planning a menu to be some kind of over-the-top stressor. I will gladly scrub down my house every Thursday morning and do three loads of laundry every day. But don't ask me to tell you what we're going to eat for dinner tomorrow night.

I don't know why it's so daunting. Unfortunately, menu planning turns out to be a key factor in inner peace in the daily home lifestyle. When you don't have a plan for dinner, five o'clock will still roll around and people will ask what's for dinner — and the thought of hitting another drive-through makes you weak with shame. I spent too many years calling my husband as he was driving home from work, asking him to pick up something for dinner. He did it, but neither of us felt good about it.

It took me years to fully understand the wisdom in putting a little time and energy into a weekly menu. If I was going to be tied up every day, either with work or with kids, I needed to have a plan in advance. Order brings peace. So I got very committed to making the weekly menu. I would plan out our meals, buy the groceries for those meals, and then make those meals. It's that easy.

There are several ways you can approach making a menu. A weekly menu makes sense for us, mostly because I can't fathom buying two weeks' worth of groceries at one time. They don't make carts big enough.

Once upon a time, I tried to do a monthly menu. The downside of this was that I was in the mood for Italian food that day, and we ended up with (I am not lying) a month of Italian dinners. As I cooked the meals that Sunday afternoon, I realized that everything I was making to freeze had a to-mato/ground beef/sausage base. I had no idea there were so many meals that were so similar. Spaghetti! Goulash! Lasagna! So for someone as uncreative in the kitchen as I am, it's best to go a week at a time. It's less overwhelming.

If you are truly desperate, you can also pay someone. For a while, I subscribed to a service that planned my weekly menu. The meals were based on the sales at the grocery store of my choice. It was a win-win situation and worked very well for the season we used it. Then, like all good things, it was time to move on. My children started to miss our "tried and true" foods, and I eventually went back to creating my own menu. But for those months that I used the menu-planning service, it was very handy and greatly appreciated.

Another idea: Send out a group text and ask everyone to reply with one dinner idea. If you have included seven people in your list, you have a weekly menu!

You can also invite friends over and make some meals together. This is a fun girls-night-in activity, and you go home with meals to put in the freezer.

At the heart of menu planning is a well-formed shopping list. Don't go grocery shopping without a list, and don't go with an empty stomach. Both approaches will cost you extra money. Plan your menu and then make a list, checking the ingredients you already have on hand and include what you need. Now that my boys are older, I also send a group text to them and my husband, asking everyone what else we need at the store. They are a font of knowledge when it comes to what we have run out of! They can even tell me how many gallons of milk we have left in the extra fridge.

The point is that learning to plan a menu will bring tremendous peace. Because no matter how much time you think you'll have on a weekday afternoon (ha!), you know deep down that you won't.

# do the laundry

*We should all do what, in the long run, gives us joy, even if it is only*
*picking grapes or sorting the laundry.*
— E. B. White

Oh, man — laundry is my jam. I love laundry, and I think, maybe with a little encouragement, you can learn to love laundry too!

Laundry often robs people of their peace. Because when laundry gets backed up, not only do we have a pile of cotton staring us down, but we also waste time looking for the clothes we need or running late because we can't find them. My children wear a uniform to school. There is nothing worse than waking up thirty minutes before they need to leave, only to discover that all the khaki pants are currently wet in the washer.

Laundry needs our attention, and it deserves our attention. The key to a happy laundry system is my personal laundry motto: A.B.H. (Always Be Hustlin').

This could also be known as: Laundry, Just Do It!

I think one of the reasons people hate laundry is because they hate putting it away. Maybe we hate putting it away because the drawers are crammed with clothes, and stuff won't easily go into them. So if you want to love doing laundry, start backwards:

1. Consider the state of your drawers. If you can't fit the clean clothes in the drawers when it's time to put things away, then it's time to purge. Set aside fifteen minutes and quickly go through the drawers to make room (for more on this, see "Purge the Clutter").
2. Put a load in the washer and then move it to the dryer. Easy enough.
3. When the clothes in the dryer are ready to come out, do NOT remove them until you are

ready to fold. This prevents clothes from piling up everywhere — unless you are one of those folks who likes having five loads of laundry to fold while you are watching your favorite show. Then proceed as usual, if that's what works for you. (Side note: Do you have a good place for storing your clean, folded laundry? This is a game changer. In my laundry room, I have carved out space for a small table that fits six small baskets. There is one basket for each of my children. This is where their laundry goes. Paul and I have a larger basket that we share, which I keep on top of the dryer.)

4. Take the laundry out of the dryer in small batches, making sure to keep it all nice and warm to fold. Everything stays wrinkle-free, and it's very soothing and therapeutic to fold. Place each item directly into the basket and walk away.

5. Repeat.

6. Repeat. And once or twice a week, have people put their laundry away.

If you don't have a table for sorting, folding, and storing, put each person's pile on the dining room table or on his or her bed. Put away small piles daily. You will get a similar result.

If I could encourage you with any part of the laundry system, it would be to fold those clothes the minute they come out of the dryer. In fact, don't take them out of the dryer until you have time to fold them. And if we're honest, it doesn't take that long to fold a load of laundry if you set your mind to it. Decide that this is the task I'm doing right now, folding this laundry.

If you prefer to watch your show while folding the last four loads of laundry, go for it. I'm not the boss of you. But, if you want laundry to be a thing that gets done, instead of an event of epic proportion, then this is how I suggest you proceed.

And just like that, getting in the habit of wiping down a bathroom, making a grocery list, and switching over laundry — giving each of these tasks their due energy and time — will simplify your life. Laundry and menu planning won't feel so epic because you've dealt with each of them (and all the other tasks of running a household) with enough energy to peacefully get the job done. And that's the key: Getting the job done. When the job is done, it isn't hanging over your head, and that mental real estate can be cleared up for other more pressing and joy-filled tasks.

chapter 2

# giving the gift of hospitality

*Hospitality is love in action. Hospitality is the flesh
and muscle on bones of love.*

— Alexander Strauch

Hospitality moves us away from a focus on ourselves and toward a focus on others. This is an important factor in peace
and order. A big part of searching for peace is a desire to hear
God's voice and to do what he needs us to do. Being God's hands
and feet means loving those around us — and it's not enough to
be nice to the person at the grocery store. We need to be open
to ministering to others by generous acts of hospitality and love.

"Hospitality," according to Wikipedia, "refers to the relationship between a guest and a host, wherein the host receives
the guest with goodwill, including the reception and enter-
tainment of guests, visitors, or strangers. Louis, chevalier de
Jaucourt describes hospitality in the *Encyclopédie* as the virtue
of a great soul that cares for the whole universe through the
ties of humanity."

Hospitality is part of the corporal works of mercy too:

To feed the hungry.

To give water to the thirsty.
To clothe the naked.
To shelter the homeless.
To visit the sick.
To visit the imprisoned or ransom the captive.
To bury the dead.

Isaiah 58:10–12 says,

> If you lavish your food on the hungry
>     and satisfy the afflicted;
> Then your light shall rise in the darkness,
>     and your gloom shall become like midday;
> Then the LORD will guide you always
>     and satisfy your thirst in parched places,
>     will give strength to your bones
> And you shall be like a watered garden,
>     like a flowing spring whose waters never fail.
> Your people shall rebuild the ancient ruins;
>     the foundations from ages past you shall raise up;
> "Repairer of the breach," they shall call you,
>     "Restorer of ruined dwellings."

Caring for others, meeting the needs of others with good-will, is not only a nice thing to do: it's part of our sanctification. The Lord asks it of us and tells us that when we feed the hungry and clothe the naked, he will strengthen us and draw us closer to him.

Hospitality is worth the effort.

As a Catholic, I think about Theology of the Body when I ponder receiving guests with goodwill. It is a gift of self and a willingness to share ourselves with others. In a practical sense, this gift of self includes inviting others into our home and being willing to share our lives.

# have company over for dinner

*If you really want to make a friend, go to someone's house and eat with him ... the people who give you their food give you their heart.*
— Cesar Chavez

I love the idea of having people over for dinner. I understand the importance of it. Hospitality is essential and good.

It's also completely overwhelming.

I'm a bit of a recovering perfectionist, and while I've made peace with the imperfections of my home, I am still hyper-aware of its flaws the minute I think about hosting guests.

But it's so important that we push through our desire to spare ourselves the time, energy, and emotional strain of allowing someone to come into our personal space and time. Thinking in those terms, hospitality is the ultimate form of vulnerability. We are allowing a part of ourselves that we are able to keep hidden from the world (the bathroom in use by my five sons comes to mind) and opening that for exposure.

Yes, it's easier to stay on friendly, safe terms with those nice folks from church but avoid getting too personal.

But the Church needs us to be real with one another. How many times have your chains of loneliness and rejection been broken by someone willing to admit to you that they, too, have problems? It's life-changing to know you aren't alone.

We are called, as Christians, to be the hands and feet of Jesus. As such, inviting people into our home, welcoming them and serving them, is an act of love. It's an opportunity not only to learn more about one another but also a chance to love, to be loved, and show love. We have people over for dinner to break down isolation (ours and theirs) and share the gift of self.

And so, I say, invite someone over to dinner. It's scary if you aren't in the habit, but you can do it. If you agree with me that you should invite someone over, but secretly you are planning to wait until the front room gets redecorated, then you need to think again. Resist the urge to put this off indefinitely.

Let's put it this way: How many times have you been invited to someone's house and been offended by their worn-out throw pillows? I'm guessing none. But we hold ourselves to a standard exponentially higher than we would hold anyone else. The times Paul and I are invited to dinner with our six children, we are simply happy to be there!

I have very fond childhood memories of an annual invitation to dinner at a neighbor's house. My parents were the godparents of this couple's son, and every year for that boy's birthday my mom and dad and all eight of us kids were invited to his party. We were such a large family, we didn't get invited to a lot of places. I absolutely loved it and can't remember anything about the food or the home decor or anything other than the joy and excitement of dining with others. I have a few other similar memories of experiencing hospitality as a child, and the sentiment is the same: being in someone else's home and feeling the love of that generous act is what matters.

You, too, can host a dinner party.

By dinner party, I simply mean invite some people to come eat food in your home. "Hosting a dinner party" sounds grand and fabulous and frightfully stressful. But translated to the reality, the act of ushering people through your front (or back) door into your home for the purpose of ingesting some food — you got this, girl!

The key to true, Christian hospitality isn't impressing people. It's not hiding all your flaws and welcoming someone into your pristine environs to show them how great your life is. Maybe you have a beautiful home, but that's not the point of having people over.

Hospitality is effective when we are willing to offer ourselves — warts and all — to build and edify the Church, the body of Christ. We break down the walls of insecurity by sharing who we really are, at our core. We stop hiding behind masks, walls, and all the other shields the world compels us to use. The world tells us life is about winning, and when life feels like a competition, you have to appear perfect. The reality of life, everyone knows deep down, is that no one is perfect. But if everyone is hiding that fact, we're all walking around being a less-true version of who we really are.

In this moment of welcoming someone into your home, you will choose to be YOU, authentic and full of life. Not a train wreck, but someone who is not afraid of being herself. Your job, as you welcome guests into your home, is to be yourself, and love, love, love. You will build up and encourage your guests because having them in your home isn't about you — it's about them. It's about the opportunity to love God's people, and to feed them a little something too.

If you feel overwhelmed at the thought of cooking for others, here's my secret: I have one wowzah meal that I know I can manage, something I've mastered that is delicious and well-received. That's what I cook every time we have people over. My Aunt Betsy has something called Chicken Dish Number Three. I guess dishes one and two are for her husband and the kids. Dish Number Three is her winner for company, and she always gets rave reviews.

For me, I stumbled upon a roast chicken that is easy and divine. It comes from Ina Garten and takes about twenty minutes to prepare. Basically, rinse the bird, stuff with garlic and lemon, set it upon a bed of carrot chunks tossed with olive oil, and coat everything with salt, pepper, and butter. You can even mess up the measurements (ask me how I know), and it will turn out *sans défaut* (sorry, dinner parties make me feel very French).

I add a family rice dish that I call "Buelo's Rice," because Paul's dad gave me the recipe from his Armenian relatives. It's a rice/browned spaghetti/bouillon combo that is also divine (simple, but also divine). I add a tossed salad, some chocolate, and several bottles of wine — and what's not to love?

Find food that is easy and delicious if the food aspect is what freaks you out. And then set your attention to all the other details that are also stressful.

Let's make a list called Hospitality Is Stressful Because:

1. The food — we got it covered! Keep it simple, or go crazy if that's your thing.
2. My children — your guests will love them, and however crazy your kids act will only make the guests love you more. You are normal! Who knew?!
3. My home — you are your own worst critic of your home. Trust me.

# host a shower

*True hospitality consists of giving the best of yourself to your guests.*
— Eleanor Roosevelt

Don't freak out, you can totally do this. For starters, think about how much it honors others that we make this effort, instead of thinking about how stressed you are about to be or how totally unworthy you are to welcome people into your home (have they seen the upstairs baseboards?!).

This is not something I'm going to force you to do, but be open to this kind of hospitality. It's a big step, an extension of the gift of self we talked about, in having people over to dinner. I've hosted lots of showers, but I always start out with self-doubt and a comparison of all the homes that would be more suitable than mine for fancy parties. And then I get over it and focus on the opportunity to provide this space for this person to get these needs met. A baby shower for a soon-to-be mother! A wedding shower for a soon-to-be wife! What beautiful, special times in a person's life! When you offer to bring people together to celebrate special times, you will be happy you made the effort. (Pro tip: Invite a friend to share the duties with you, and it will be even more fun!)

My friend Aunt Harriett is a caterer, so whenever I host an event I call her and ask her to go over the menu with me. She helps distill the moving parts into something less overwhelming. If you are new to hosting a shower, I would advise you to avoid going down the black hole that is Pinterest. Seek as much inspiration as you want, but keep in mind that people will remember the warmth and generosity you offered your guests more than your cleverly color-coded decor. For me, when I keep things simple, I am a happy hostess who enjoys the gathering.

Aunt Harriett always recommends something sweet (like a cake or cookies); fruit, like a platter of strawberries and grapes; something salty, like nuts, pretzels, or vegetables with a dip. You should also offer water, tea or coffee, and some kind of punch or wine. Aunt Harriett gave me the best advice when I was stressing out about how much food to provide: Remember, this will not be anyone's last meal! We offer the food for people to enjoy, but ultimately it's all about the person we are honoring, and about this honored guest getting the items they need to start this next new adventure of life.

# host an overnight guest
*The surest way to determine whether one possesses*
*the love of God is to see whether he or she loves his or her neighbor.*
*These two loves are never separated.*
— Saint Teresa of Ávila

Did you freak out just now? Me too. I will admit, having people spend the night at our house is not my favorite. I'm especially talking about little kids.

I won't spend a lot of time here on spend-the-nights, kids' version, except to say they are overrated. The kids get no sleep, and the adults get even less. We have found that not doing those kinds of sleepovers brings us a lot of peace. Our kids know that this is our family standard, and it works for us. If you find yourself hesitant to indulge your kids in the requested sleepover, allow yourself to say NO. You are allowed to tell your kids that you as a family don't do sleepovers. We've gone so far as to let friends come over and play until 11 p.m. — and then drive them home. Best of both worlds!

But beyond that, let's talk about hosting overnight guests of the grown-up variety. Guests in need of a place to stay brings hospitality to a whole new level. It also brings vulnerability to a whole new level.

Regardless of whether you have a perfect guest suite or not, everyone struggles with overnight hospitality to some degree. I've been in a friend's (perfect!) home and been surprised to hear her point out the flaws of the house, not quite apologizing but acknowledging what could be better. While I was surprised to hear that she thought anything needed improvement (it looks so lovely!), I realized we all have some area about our home we would love to improve. So move forward, knowing that even the people with the most perfect home have something they want to fix. Don't wait to host someone until your house is perfect.

Overnight guests are tricky because you can only hide your crazy for so long. When you invite someone to stay overnight in your home, you run the risk of them realizing you aren't perfect! And that, my friend, is what's so great about this kind of hospitality.

## handle the holidays with peace
*Peace begins with a smile.*
— Saint Teresa of Calcutta

Now that you've successfully hosted someone for dinner and hosted a shower (or thought about how feasible that will be for you), let's talk about the holidays. The word "peace" is often mentioned within the Christmas season, but how many of us find it's not always present? We have to work so hard to maintain sanity in the holiday season, much less have peace. But if we want peace, we must go after it, knowing what we are up against.

One study on the holidays found them to be most stressful on women, particularly because much of the hosting, planning, and preparation falls to us. Who is surprised to hear this? We want to handle the holidays with grace and peace, but we also have to make the season joy-filled for our families and extended relatives.

Here's how:

1. Start by knowing your limitations. You can't do all the things in all the ways. Admit this to yourself, and recognize that you will need to set limits.

2. Divide the work — especially when it comes to hosting for your larger, extended family. Be willing to let others help. This will mean letting go of some control (must you micromanage what kind of rolls are on the table?). In my family, we tend to set general guidelines of what food we would like to have and text the list to everyone. People reply with what they are going to bring, and then we fill in the gaps with specific requests. (Side note: Rolls can always go to that single brother of yours — not sexist, just trying to get the job done.)

3. Don't be a martyr. It's painful. Accept help, be at peace. You need to enjoy the holidays as much as anyone else. Your family needs you to, also. At one particularly long holiday gathering, my dad offered to help with some aspect of service, and I remember telling him, "No, I have to do it; it's my job," and I felt this little spot of pity in my soul. Ridiculous! Accept help and everyone will have a happier time.

4. Don't rely on alcohol to get you through. One day I'll tell you about the time I let a family member refill my glass of peppermint schnapps

until everything seemed warm and hazy. The day did not end well. Another family member got upset about something, and I was not in a position to bring peace by letting go and letting God. I addressed the situation in my schnapps-fueled state of being. Don't do this.

5. Don't forget to serve alcohol. Wait, what? A glass of wine might make you a better host. Find something that helps you take a deep breath, avoid the temptation to be a martyr, and remember to welcome everyone into your home with the peace and joy you yourself would like to receive. Maybe go for a run or read a chapter of a book before everyone arrives. Focus on being at peace with yourself, and with those around you, and the memories will be happier for all involved.

# be hospitable to yourself

*There is nothing more miserable in the world than to arrive in paradise and look like your passport photo.*
— Erma Bombeck

One last way to bring peace to our home is through hospitality to ourselves. You are often the most overlooked person in your life.

Take a minute to consider your own personal space within your home. You can bring peace to yourself by giving that area some TLC, providing a relaxing space to enter at the end of your day caring for others. Within your own bedroom, what can you do to simplify and fill it with warmth and peace?

1. Avoid letting your bedroom become the gathering place of all the other junk in the house. Yes, you want the more visible areas to be tidy, but avoid your room being filled to the rafters with

everyone else's junk. Take some time to purge
your room and remove from the space anything
that doesn't belong there. If the room is filled
with stuff that doesn't have a home, find a home
for it! Just not on the floor of your bedroom.

2. Get some nice bedding. You don't need Egyptian
cotton to make things nice. These days there is so
much lovely bedding at affordable prices. For true
*hygge* effect, have a nice comforter, pretty pillows,
two pillows with shams, and a folded blanket at
the foot of the bed. Add a side table with space for
a lamp, maybe a candle, a few books. (For more
information about *hygge*, see pages 78 and 79.)

3. In your bathroom, consider an updated shower curtain for an instant boost. Also, make sure
you do not accumulate all the ratty towels for
you and your husband. Nice bath towels, hand
towels, and bath mats make the space clean and
cozy. I also recently invested in a fake plant for
my bathroom counter, and it's ridiculous how
much joy that thing has brought me.

4. I've gone back and forth about having a television
in our room. As my boys started getting older,
and I found myself needing a space to "retreat"
to when I needed a break, I gave serious thought
to getting a TV. I pushed through and didn't get
one, and now I enjoy the space as being quiet
and restful. It's not device-free because, for better or for worse, we have our smartphones. But
having the space clear of clutter and welcoming
to me (and my husband) is important.

5. Finally, don't let your family overtake your
room! Have boundaries. Allow your children to
be as welcome as you would like, but don't feel
bad if you want this space to remain off limits to
everyone but mom and dad.

chapter 3

# peace through organization

*A place for everything, and everything in its place.*
— Proverb

If you want your home to be tidy and easy to pick up, you do need to have a place for everything. This can be as complicated or simple as you need. Look around your home right now. What is robbing you of your peace? What are the items that seem impossible to organize? What spaces seems overwhelming to keep tidy? Those are your "problem" areas — and don't fret. If you answered "every single space in this whole house," it's going to be okay.

When you want a house that is easy to keep clean and tidy, you have to be honest with the amount of time and energy you are willing to invest on an hourly, daily, and weekly basis. This is a judgement-free statement. A very dear friend once told me that she knows she doesn't have the time, energy, or interest to keep a house perfectly picked up. That's valid and acceptable. The only person you have to answer to about your home is you, and maybe your spouse. The two of you should certainly try to be on the same page when it comes to standards in the home — and that can work both ways. You might be part of a couple who would much rather sit and relax and deal with washing the dishes later. If that works for you both and brings peace, do that. I knew a woman who could move a giant pile of laundry to the side and invite her friends to sit and watch a movie. The mess didn't bother her one bit.

But if that's the way things are but not how you would like them to be, there are some options!

The heart of successful organization is the ability to divide and conquer. If you are staring out at a sea of flotsam — in your home, your paperwork, your daily schedule, and the list goes on — let's break it down and then break those parts into smaller parts. Before long, you will find a subsection of your home and life that you can order, and that will bring you peace.

## purge the clutter

*She is rich who has a forty pack of one-gallon ziplocks.*
— Rachel Balducci

The hardest part about organization is all the stuff we have to organize. The good news is, the less stuff you have, the less you will have to organize. It seems like a no-brainer, but we forget this!

The first step in true home organization is a willingness to declutter.

If you are feeling at a complete loss, start by reading Marie Kondo's *The Life-Changing Magic of Tidying Up*. It's a game changer and a quick read. My takeaways from reading that book are: (1) it is so important to emotionally let go of items around your house, and (2) you must have a fierce commitment to having less stuff. You have to attack the junk if you want to be free of it.

To have a deep, clean, intense purge, start with a very small space. Don't tackle organizing your kitchen; tackle organizing this one drawer in your kitchen. When you are done with that drawer (or maybe three of the drawers), you can move on to another space, maybe the lower cabinets. Don't set out to organize your entire bedroom; organize your closet, and then move on to the drawers of your dresser. Keep the project contained and set limits so that you don't get overwhelmed. Also, keep in mind that this will be painful and exhausting (or fun and pain-free?). But if you are thorough and honest, you are giving yourself the gift that keeps on giving: less stuff means less stuff to put away. If you are brutal with your clutter, you won't have to do this again in the near future.

Take out all the items of this space. And then don't put anything back into that space that you don't absolutely love, need, or use.

This will not be the organizations of times gone by, where you shuffled everything and put it back in a new order. This is going to be the time you get rid of that dress you've been keeping that looks terrible on you but you keep anyway because you, and only you, remember what you spent on that dress. This will be the time you find the courage to donate those shoes you found on sale from the magazine you love, the ones that hurt your feet but are super cute (and you got such a great deal!). It's time to get rid of any single thing in all of these spaces that doesn't serve some very useful purpose and also bring you great joy.

Sometimes we keep things that do the opposite. For years, I held on to clothes and dishes and other items because I should, in theory, like them or use them or at least have them in my home. But I didn't, and those items simply took up space in my home, preventing clearer shelves, drawers, and space for me to think, breathe, and keep my house clean.

My experience with this deep purge was indeed life-changing. I spent several weeks and tackled a small section every day. I would pull out all of those items and think about what I wanted to keep. One kooky and amazing thing Ms. Kondo has you do is thank the items that you decide not to keep. I laughed at this idea until I tried it, but it helped me let go of things I had held on to for years. Instead of keeping the dress that should have been my favorite, I thanked it for the joy it brought me while I was waiting for it to come in the mail. And I thanked it for teaching me the important lesson of not buying expensive clothes online without free shipping. Some of the boys' old baby clothes needed to be donated. I thanked those clothes for the memories and for keeping my sweet babies warm and cozy.

Some items are very difficult to let go. And if you absolutely can't figure out how, maybe that's an item that needs to stay. You don't need to get rid of every single thing (you actually shouldn't!). But an amazing freedom comes with this letting go. The act of letting go frees your soul to focus less on all the stuff in your life and more on the freedom of a clean, light space ready for peace-filled living.

Once you've dropped off your giant black garbage bags of stuff to be donated (this will take several trips), you can more easily begin the fine art of organizing what you do have left.

Good organization is about putting like things together. And this concept of "like things" can vary with each person. Maybe like items for you are all your green articles of clothing or all of the red foods in your fridge. Or maybe it's all of the cold-weather items in one drawer or all the eye makeup in a small bin. Pay attention to what seems logical to you. In my closet, I group my clothes by type (dresses, then skirts, then shirts). I tried arranging items by color, and it looked much prettier, but over time I went back to my tried-and-true method.

In my children's rooms, we limit the amount of junk they can keep. At least when they are younger and still learning about hanging on to things, I work on giving them a container where all the extra stuff can go. If it doesn't fit in there, they need to shuffle what they have, either getting rid of old stuff to make room for the new or not holding on to the new at all. Instead of feeling obliged to find space for all the things, decide what things are allowed to be in your space. What do you want your bedrooms to look like? Have an image of that and make your stuff fit into that plan.

When you give each space in your home this kind of thoughtful approach, mindful of what is there and what is truly needed, you will move out of a home filled with "just because" stuff into a home containing what you need, want, and take great pleasure in having.

My friend Carrie has a theory that people like shopping at Target because everything there is neat and organized, with bins and containers everywhere. So we buy up those bins and bring them home, thinking we will find the organization and order we seek. But that creates more items that need a place to go. The key is to avoid buying any more bins and start getting rid of the piles of things gathering around your home.

# organize your time
*Time is what we want most, but what we use worst.*
— William Penn

In her book *A Mother's Rule of Life*, Holly Pierlot contemplates the order we need in our homes for peace. At the end of her book, she offers the reader a daily schedule that is mapped out in thirty-minute increments. She includes ideas for weekly, daily, and hourly tasks for herself and her children. It's impressive what she is able to manage by paying such close attention to her time and days. She has a sense of what activities are on the horizon and what jobs need to get done when.

Years ago, I spent a few nap times studying that book. I wanted so badly to recreate this level of organization in my day, in my home. I needed more order in our hours than we currently had, and I hoped that I could simply cut and paste what she had offered in her book to make it work for my family.

I could not.

Despite my best efforts, having my day planned out down to the minute took more energy than I had. Instead of that schedule serving me, I was serving it. After giving it my very best effort over the course of several weeks, I realized that what I could receive from that book was the inspiration to come up with a schedule, and the wisdom to determine a schedule for the Family Balducci. Her schedule was beautiful and inspired, and I could glean from it the importance of putting time and energy into ordering my time and energy.

Only you will know what works best for you. You need to find a daily schedule, a system for work, chores charts and routines — and all of this needs to be a method that fits into your own particular madness. Some people need a very fluid and open-ended approach to the day. Anything tighter than that will cause anxiety or stress. Some people, myself included, · need a sense of plan before the day gets started. If I know at least by breakfast what we will do that morning, this is helpful to me. Of course, with smaller children I had more open blocks on my daily schedule. These days our calendar includes many activities, and my job is to fit in regular life around sports and scholastic practices and events. Life with bigger children is wonderful, but it takes a level of planning finesse.

To-do lists are our best friend, and it's important to keep several lists. What do you need to get done this week? What do you need to get done today? And what do you need to get done during this chunk of the day? Looking to the bigger picture of the week, or two or three days in advance, will help us avoid living at the level of minute-by-minute existence. Sometimes, emergency response is the best we can do — and in crazy times, I honestly can't handle much more than twenty-four hours in advance. I might know everything we have going on, but no real way to manage it too far ahead.

However, when we are able to slow down enough to catch our breath, take a breather and think (even for five to seven minutes) about what's coming up, we can make some plans that will save us some grief.

*"Prior Planning Prevents Poor Performance."*

I grew up with my dad saying this mantra over and over. And it's true! The great thing is that each of us can decide how much prior planning she needs to find peace. Talk about the calendar with your spouse, even if your official "calendar planning meeting" is the two of you standing in the kitchen for three minutes before you leave for the day. This will save the heartache of discovering that you never actually told your spouse out loud that you needed him to pick up the carpool. The stress that comes from hauling across town because you failed to find someone to pick up your son from his swim practice, well, that kind of excitement is something I'd like to experience as little as possible.

Do what works best for your family. (Are you seeing a recurring theme here?)

Chore charts are a similar organizational tool that is unique to every household.

My experience with chore charts runs the spectrum. I grew up with a very organized mom who loved charts. She had a chart for meals, for snacks, for our daily schedule, and for chores. For years, this was the standard that I wanted to attain. I wanted to have my entire week of food planned, written, and posted. It's important to consider how your children function, but at the heart of every good organizational system is the person who has created the system because it works best for her. Once I made peace with my freedom and declared that I could not recreate my mother's system, I took the pressure off myself. I was finally able to consider the point of chore charts, which is to bring peace to a home and to train a child in the way he should go, per Proverbs 22:6, so that he will not depart from it when he gets old.

More than a nicely color-coded chore chart, you want children trained in the art of order and peace. A friend of mine shared about a meeting she had with her child's doctor. The child was learning how to keep his room clean, and the doctor was reviewing with my friend why we even take the time to train our children. It's not just about learning to be organized, the two of them discussed, but the act of showing love to those around us. Bringing order shows love because it says, "I want to help in this situation; I want to be a part of the solution." Order is also an important part of physical and mental health.

This reminded me of the importance of proactively training children. Maybe it's not enough to assign as we go. Children need to have an understanding of the tasks that are theirs, their daily responsibilities.

Eventually, after the attempts at lavish charts, and then swinging completely to the other side with everyone always pitching in together, I decided to have a finite list for each child. Yes, we work together as a family to get the job done, but each child must understand how to be a part of the daily "solution" of running the household.

I came up with the solution that each child is responsible for his little part of our world. That means he keeps his room clean (with my help of knowing what our standard is). He puts away his laundry, and he keeps an eye on his laundry basket to know when to do that. He is responsible for putting his dirty clothes where they go and keeping the system of cleanliness moving forward.

This is very simple, isn't it? On paper, maybe it's not a lot of responsibility. I decided that I want my children to have a handful of things they do that they learn to do really well. My standard for cleanliness in our home includes clutter-free bedrooms, and the kids are learning how to manage that. I think that's a life skill worth investing in.

In the bigger picture, after several attempts, I've found that it's best to ask each child to help in the way that will best serve me and the family in that moment. One evening, that might mean loading the dishwasher or setting the table. Another evening, that might mean I clean the kitchen while everyone else tackles a room to pick up.

To me, the key is to teach the family to help run the household. I don't do well when I'm cleaning and everyone is sitting around relaxing. I understand the mom will always have something to do, some project or task that needs attention. But the best training a child can get is to be aware of what is happening around him and to be willing to pitch in. If someone around you is working hard, be willing to be a part of the solution.

I'm always quick to point out that when we work together the job gets done quickly, and then we can all go back to the art of enjoying the moment.

Whatever method you find, remember that the end goal is to train your children. You are teaching them to pursue peace and order by helping bring these things to your home right now. Find something that is easy for you to commit to so that you can help your children commit.

## say no
*We must learn the art of setting limits.*
— Richard Swenson, M.D.

We live in a world of overload.

In *Margin*, Dr. Swenson lists manifestations of the overload syndrome. They include overloads in activity, choice, commitment, debt, decision, expectation, noise, people, technology, traffic, and even hurry. "God did not create hurry," writes Dr. Swenson.

When my children were little, I had a nice excuse to say no to a lot of things. You can't drag four little boys to too much without it costing you your sanity and also your pride.

So early on as a mother, my default answer was no. I couldn't go to that particular park (not enough fencing) or that restaurant (too much glass) or even things like daily Mass (too much silence).

In those days, I made life decisions based on what the Balducci boys could handle or, more importantly, if the amount of training and redirecting was worth the effort. Of course, we will go to Sunday Mass, I reasoned, but that was my limit. The effort to keep so many little boys quiet and behaved was worth going through about once a week.

But as the boys got older and more mobile, I found that

saying yes became a little easier. We could go places and do things. And once the boys were big enough to behave, that afforded even more fun outside the home.

I remember my first experience with this. The older boys had started school, and I was down to having only one boy at home with me. Augie was three at that point and was my little pal. His three older brothers were all in elementary school, and I could do things like go to daily Mass and volunteer. If Augie could come with me, we were good to go.

Around that time a new priest came to our parish, and he was a go-getter. He had many amazing things happening, and I was excited to help. And then I volunteered to teach Spanish at the boys' school (two hours a week) and to be on a team developing talks on Christian living. So many fun, exciting things I had never been able to do before, and my boys getting bigger opened doors for me!

But just like that, after saying yes and yes and yes, I hit a wall. Even though all of it was good, I had to admit that I was doing too much.

After completing a few of the commitments, I opted to scale back, and I realized that I needed to look at the calendar differently. Just because an hour was open didn't mean I needed to squeeze something in.

It's so easy to get in the habit of saying yes, but that quickly (oh, so quickly!) snowballs into overload. I focused too much on the joy of service and forgot to consider that I can't do everything.

Saying yes to God doesn't mean saying yes to everything. Learn to say no.

I started by not saying yes to anything right off the bat. Instead I'd say, "Let me talk with Paul and get back with you."

Now if that sounds olden-timey chauvinistic, that's okay. For me, using my husband to help protect me from overload is one of the smartest things I've ever done. First off, Paul isn't actually making the decision for me. He's there to let me talk through the pros and cons of saying yes (or no!). Also, he tends to provide good feedback. And mostly, it buys me time. That's a good habit. Usually people who struggle with burnout get there because of an inclination to say yes right away.

Now you're probably thinking back to the first part of this book, all about the epic burnout that got me rethinking the concept of peace and order and simplicity. So, yes, learning to say no is a constant battle for some of us. It's okay to admit that we might not get this perfectly right every single time. There will be ebb and flow, but hopefully each round of doing too much and scaling back will get us a little closer to center target.

It's important to serve, and it's important to stretch yourself. It's also totally acceptable to say no. Finding a balance is important. Some of us might struggle with saying no too often and need to be stretched to do a little more. But more likely, you are someone who says yes, yes, yes, and it's probably at the cost of your sanity and family.

Be honest with yourself on both ends of the spectrum, and be at peace. When you say no, it gives someone else a chance to step up and help get the job done.

part II

# personal order

*Almost everything will work again if you*
*unplug it for a few minutes, including you.*
— Anne Lamott

Personal order means taking care of OURSELVES. It's self-care, which is an important concept. There is a lot of talk about self-care because it needs to be discussed. Women are good about taking care of other people but not always good about following through and caring for themselves.

Some of the suggestions in this section might seem silly. My eyebrows? Really?

But hear me out! Taking care of the little things in our life, little ways of paying attention to details and making time to deal with them, really does make a difference. Paying attention to the details allows us to deal with them and move on. You won't need to spend any time fretting over some random pain in your mouth because you've been to the dentist recently, and you know that all is well. You won't need to spend time trying to get your face to look the way you want because you've taken the time to manage that hair and skin, and you are ready to move on to more important issues!

And so, self-care, personal order, is less about making ourselves the center of the universe and more about giving this part of our life its due. It's taking care of a few details, and then getting on to the real business of life.

chapter 4

# have peace about your body

*Beauty will save the world!*
— Fyodor Dostoyevsky

This section is going to feel counterintuitive, maybe even weird. How can my desire for a simple life include thinking about myself? Shouldn't simplicity be thinking about less, maybe even nothing?

But strangely enough, the opposite is true. Simplicity and peace and order actually involve giving the many moving parts of our life their proper due. Spending the right amount of time on the right things cultivates simplicity. It brings us order, which brings us peace.

In an effort to streamline or simplify, we might be tempted to not deal with certain things. Many of the items in this next section are easy for us to forgo. But I have found that not taking care of these seemingly silly items has caused me more problems than the freedom I thought I gain by avoiding them.

Have you ever looked in the mirror to discover you are falling apart at the seams? And then you start to think about the passage of time, how life goes on, and that you might as well get used to that old, worn-out gal staring back at you, but that God loves you anyway — and vanity, all is vanity. And then you remember to go get your hair trimmed, and you remember that you are not an octogenarian yet, and that it's going to be okay.

Honestly, ignoring some things actually makes me think about them a whole lot more.

We can't ignore things just because we don't want to use our precious time to deal with them. This applies to big things like balancing a checkbook and getting the oil changed, and smaller things like having a nice smile and a well-groomed coif.

Now the fact that I need to explain myself here proves my point. I have also gone through seasons where taking care of myself was too easy to put off, because who has the time or the money or the patience? Between you and me, getting my nails done is about as much fun as getting a mammogram. In each case, you are locked into someone else's control for an extended period of time, having someone you don't know up in space that's deeply personal. (Actually, when I put it that way, mammograms are much easier and take about one-tenth of the time.)

We certainly need to be careful to avoid an emphasis on our wants and needs that distracts from our focus. We have to spend more time gazing on the beauty of God and his love for us than on the things we could be doing better or how we are a hot mess. So keep that in mind as you think through how to take better care of yourself. Everything in moderation.

But I can offer this section because I'm confident that most of us struggle more with not taking care of our personal needs than taking too much care. How many of us have gotten a little money for our birthday and used it for something extravagant — like a new booster seat for the toddler? Let's pay attention to ourselves so that we can quit thinking about ourselves so much.

# get a haircut, deal with your eyebrows

*Time marches on and sooner or later*
*you realize it's marchin' across your face.*
— Truvy, in *Steel Magnolias*

My friend Bridgit is a hairdresser. She knows the importance of a good haircut and sees the difference it makes in her clients. There's something important about taking care of this small, seemingly frivolous detail because somehow, when you are walking around with a good haircut, you can take your mind off yourself and focus on other things. She said that when her regulars come in for a quick tune-up, there is an immediate change.

"A haircut gives them just enough boost and sparkle to feel confident and not so defeated," said Bridgit. "I file it under 'if you can't change how you feel, change how you look!'"

A good haircut can change how you look and how you feel. How many times have you gone too long between a cut and color only to find yourself working through feelings of sadness and ennui? Maybe they are minimal feelings, but they're there. You find yourself searching for consolation from the Lord because you are getting older and you need to learn to age gracefully. You are falling apart, and it shows, and you want Jesus to help you learn to deal with it.

But you aren't falling apart. You just need a trim.

"I have said this so many times," said Bridgit. "There is nothing worse than trying to be a Christian witness of how amazing motherhood is to others and looking like motherhood has defeated you in sudden death overtime. Sometimes a pretty hairstyle and a little lipstick can be a game changer."

I tend to fall into thinking that spending time on my looks is vanity. If I'm not careful, I can start to get a little prideful about how I strike the right balance in my appearance self-care. But it's still pride if we pride ourselves as much on our lack of attention instead of an obsession with our looks.

Resist the temptation to look at the beauty parlor as the

slippery slope to moral turpitude. Like the oxygen mask that drops down on a plane, you have to take care of yourself before tending to those around you. I can go on and on about how there should moderation with this, but the truth is, as mothers, we tend to swing far in the direction of caring for our kids first. How many times do you get your kids haircuts? And yourself? There. I proved my point. We are slow to put our needs before those of our children, so I'm not worried about you abusing this section.

There is such peace in doing small acts of self-care. Getting your brows waxed is easy to put off. I am Swedish and don't have tons of facial hair. But when I put off this simple act, it makes me spend too much time fretting about looking right. "What in the world is going on?" I ask, as I repeatedly spend too much time in front of the mirror, trying to get my brows to behave themselves. I'm wasting so much energy! But I convince myself I don't need to go, and I don't have the time (it literally takes four minutes), or I don't want to spend the money (less than twenty dollars). And then I go, my face looks right again, and it's one less thing in life competing for my attention. Take care of these little things, and then you'll have time for something much more important.

Get a haircut. It will change your outlook on life. You aren't falling apart at the seams after all. And if you are? Hey, now you'll look fabulous doing it.

## take care of business

*Be true to your teeth and they won't be false to you.*

— Soupy Sales

The tough thing about being a grown-up is how, generally, no one forces us to do things we don't want to do. When it comes down to the things we "need" to do, it's mind over matter. Paying the water bill is easy because we need water. We are motivated by the joy and beauty of running water in the home. This might seem like a strange thing to take note of (who doesn't pay their water bill?!) — but there are people out there who get too busy or distracted or frenzied to pay the water bill. True story: When I was a young mama with a Suburban-load of toddlers and babies, I thought the kind people at the utilities department would take into consideration that I was completely overwhelmed: *I didn't pay last month because I had too many other things to do. And you've sent me this bill with a giant piece of orange paper included, but I know you know that I'm actually a nice, cute person who will totally pay this bill when I feel like it.*

When people don't get their money, stuff gets turned off. It's a mathematical equation called "Being A Grown-Up," and it's a quick and painful one to learn.

We can get away with avoiding other areas of our life. Like a mammogram, or going to the dentist.

I put off going to the dentist for many years because for some dumb reason I thought that pregnant women can't get their teeth cleaned. If I had stopped to think, I would have figured out how crazy that is. When I finally sat in the chair after back-to-back-to-back babies, I was in bad shape. Instead of taking care of myself with regular cleanings, I had let a few years go by, and there was work to be done. That turned going to the dentist into a scary, mind-over-matter event, because instead of a fun-filled cleaning it was the less fun, face-numbing drilling.

Not taking care of what we should take care of costs us something. I guarantee you, the more time I spent putting off taking care of things — my water bill, getting my teeth cleaned, dealing with paperwork around the house — the less peace I had. I knew I was out of order, and changing that behavior took some real effort.

My mom has had breast cancer twice. This information never bothered me personally; it's always been more about the suffering she has endured as a result. But a few years ago, my life was out of order in the stress department, and when it came

time for my annual exam I found myself barely able to function. Suddenly, because I was so depleted emotionally from all
the other things I had going on, my sensory nervous system
decided that going to see my doctor was the most dangerous,
scary thing in the world. I checked in, and the nurse was con-
cerned by my blood pressure. "It's just because I'm here," I had
to admit. So embarrassing.

When it was finally time for me to see the doctor, I broke
down in heaving sobs. The pressure and anxiety were too much.

"I feel like I'm a ticking time-bomb with my health," I
admitted. I didn't realize that's how I felt until I was crying on
the exam table.

"What's going on?" he asked, and we went from there.

Knowledge is power. While I would have preferred to skip
that appointment, it was clear, based on the amount of fear and
anxiety that had crept in, that I needed to do something about
it. The mammogram wasn't painless, but the peace of mind,
knowing that whatever ache and pain I might be suffering was
harmless, was worth what it took for me to go into that office.
No one holds your hand and walks you into these places, but if
that's what you need, call a friend. For my first mammogram,
my friend Susie scheduled hers and told me we should go together. So we did, and we survived. It's hard being a grown-
up and having to do the hard thing. But the peace that comes
with taking care of business is what we need. Ignoring the water bill only makes the water go away, nothing else. Simplicity
lies in doing, not ignoring.

# go shopping
*"Treat yo'self."*
— Donna and Tom, in *Parks and Recreation*

How many times have you been given a little cash or a gift
card and bought something for your kids? (Raising hand.) It's
not crazy or a bad thing to want to take care of our people. But

if we get in the habit of never thinking about ourselves, we can quickly get in a tired, sad little state of "Woe is me" without even realizing we've sunk so low.

So go shopping! And if you faint at the thought, I guarantee it's time for you to have a stroll through a store and think only about yourself. Selfish! Shameful! Indulgent!

One day I experienced an episode of "shopping bulimia." I walked through the store and put every item that caught my fancy into my cart. I was at one of those glorious big-box stores, so there was a wide range to choose from. By the end, I had grabbed several shirts, some lotion, a few items for my home, and office supplies in the latest decorated motif. And then, instead of heading to the checkout, I walked back through the store and put everything back. I had the joy of finding fun new things and the joy of not losing money at the cash register. Hear me out: I'm not a proponent of retail therapy for the therapy alone. That's fun, but there is, literally, a price to pay. Also, I have been known to talk myself out of purchases by fast-forwarding a few months and imagining those same items going into the basket I keep on hand for Goodwill donations.

But there is something to be said for taking time to get new things. It keeps us from getting in a rut; it keeps our sense of perspective. Shopping helps practically and emotionally.

I realized one day, as I was getting ready to leave the house, that I hadn't gone clothes shopping for myself in several years. While I was teaching full-time, I had a dress code that made getting ready every morning nice and easy. My only purchases had been of the blue/white oxford shirt/khaki skirt variety.

After I stopped teaching, I found myself fretting every time I had somewhere to be. I realized it had been so long since I bought something "cute" that it was actually demanding time and energy each morning. Simplicity in that situation meant finding one of those amazing "Everything is 40 percent off!" sales and treating myself to a few new blouses and pants.

Now when I leave the house, it doesn't take all the time and energy it once did.

Clothes shopping is fun, but shopping for your home is even better!

For better or for worse, I visited my sister when she was three-weeks post-partum and about to move. That meant I came into a home that was always ready for potential buyers. It also meant that Joanna had done a crazy amount of cleaning and organizing and tiny little *hygge* (the Danish concept of cozy, happy living) touches because she had recently been in a nesting phase, and also, she needed to sell her house.

I walked into this perfection, leaving my own world behind for a few days. I was at the season of "I'm currently working too many hours outside the home, and I have a bunch of teenage sons, and it's also basketball season, and we're at the gym all the time." It was a tale of two dwellings.

I returned determined to fall back in love with my home. I wanted to like being in my home, I wanted to feel good about my family being in this space. I wanted to reinvent the whole thing without spending what I thought it could take to do all of these things.

Simplicity at its core is being content and happy with your surroundings and not having to spend energy working through the deep emotional burden of what kind of horrible person hates everything about her home?

Usually, I can overcome these feelings with a deep house cleaning. But sometimes too much time has passed, and I need to add a few little touches that help me love my environment. It doesn't take much.

This time, I decided I could make it happen.

Before I headed out to the store, I made a deliberate walk-through of my home. What little areas could use sprucing? What small touches could I make to feel warmth and love?

In his book *The Little Book of Hygge*, Meik Wiking talks about the little touches we can give our home that make it comfortable and cozy. This is decorating not for the sake of having a house that looks cute but for providing a space for your loved ones to feel nurtured and cared for.

"*Hygge* is about an atmosphere and an experience, rather than about things," writes Wiking. "It is about being with the people we love. A feeling of home. A feeling that we are safe, that we are shielded from the world and allow ourselves to let our guard down."

What I really wanted was not cutesy new things to fill my home, but a reset. I needed to focus on creating a space for my people where we could simply be. Part of that was helping me rekindle a love for the space itself — letting go of all the feelings of not liking my house and the way those feelings crept into so many other areas of life.

Taking my cue from my post-nesting house-on-the-market sister, I paid attention to the details. I got nice hand soaps and new hand towels for the bathrooms. I got a candle for the kitchen. At an upscale consignment shop, I found a pair of throw pillows for the couch that transformed the front room. I also got new coir doormats for the entryways, an electric teakettle for the kitchen, and a new table runner for the dining room.

For a few hundred dollars, I ended up with what felt like a whole new home. It was exciting and fun, and it changed my whole outlook on my house. This exercise in coziness also reminded me of the importance of making the effort for my family. There are so many demands on our time and attention; but for these people, our little domestic church, this is the best use of it all.

## fall in love with exercise

*Exercise gives you endorphins. Endorphins make you happy. Happy people just don't shoot their husbands, they just don't.*
— Elle Woods, in *Legally Blonde*

Exercise helps you not want to murder your family. Seriously. It's so good.

Of course, you can set some personal goals as well. Run a 5K. Walk a 5K. Maybe do a half marathon. Maybe get to the gym three days this week. You will be glad you did. Your problems will fall into perspective.

Exercise can feel so epic. If you are in the habit of lifting weights or running, you can't imagine missing a day. If you are out of the habit, you can't imagine you have the time. It's all about effort. Exercise simplifies life because it solves so many problems. People who exercise are healthier, happier, have a better outlook on life, have fewer medical issues, and generally sleep better too. When you make the time to get in a workout, even a simple twenty-minute exercise video or walk around the track, you are helping yourself physically and mentally.

In my love affair with exercise, I've had some highs and lows. Puberty was not kind to me. I was that teenage girl who woke up one day thirty pounds heavier than she had been in seventh grade. I hate pictures of myself from high school (except my giant hair was amazing — thank you, Aqua Net!). I discovered the gym when I was in college and got hooked. Around that same time, I also started running, and that combo helped me feel fit, happy, and great about life.

In those years after Paul and I got married and I had four babies in five years, exercise kept me sane. I got up at 5 a.m. for years and hit the gym. It didn't hurt that I was in my twenties and had energy to spare.

After I had Henry and Isabel (both at the "advanced maternal age" of late thirties), it was harder to get the weight off. I started running when Henry was a toddler, and I was actually training for a half marathon when I discovered Isabel was on the way. I tried getting right back into running after she was born, but the grace was gone, as they say.

That was a hard season for me. I had to work hard to love exercise again. I had no time or energy for long runs, and hitting the gym didn't work like it used to. After several years, Paul and I started an exercise program that got the weight off, and it reminded me of the joys of that endorphin rush.

My friend Stacey is a personal trainer, and she has seen first-hand what it means for a person to make the decision to move in the direction of getting healthy. But it's a hard first step.

"I most often see how nervous people are to just start," she said. "And I remind them to do only what they can do and don't look at what anyone else is doing."

She said for many people who are out of the habit of working out, getting into the habit can be scary and daunting.

"I say getting in the door is the hardest part," she said, adding that she tells people that if they just get themselves to the gym, she will take good care of them. "Every small effort has its victory, whether it's being able to do one more rep, or go a little deeper into a squat, or walk a little further."

It doesn't take long for people who were once over-whelmed and intimidated by exercise to start loving it. She notices quick changes in a person's self-confidence and their desire to keep going. But, in the words of Lao-tzu, "The journey of a thousand miles begins with a single step."

"My standard go-to advice," said Stacey, "is that you find something you enjoy doing so that it doesn't feel like a chore. Then you'll want to do it. If running isn't your thing, try hiking. Find a buddy to work out with, because you are going to enjoy it more with a friend, and you can hold each other accountable to doing it."

She recommends that you start slow and work up, because if you go too hard too fast you may be too sore to continue, or feel defeated and never go back.

Don't focus on how far you have to go to reach your goals. Put one foot in front of the other. There is no time like the present — and you can see why all the athletic people have this kind of rhetoric! It's about getting your brain to get on board with what your body needs. If you are overwhelmed at the thought of all this, find a mentor. Talk to a friend who is in the habit of working out, and find the motivation you need. Set goals for yourself, and focus on how good you are going to feel, not how bad it's going to hurt!

"Exercise is crucial for stress relief, energy, and mental health," said Stacey. "Continuing to build bone and muscle as we age is so important. Start slow and then you'll see the benefits, and then it becomes a must-have part of your routine."

But exercise alone can't solve all your problems. If you're wanting to lose a few or more than a few pounds, you have to consider what you eat.

"It doesn't matter how much you work out," Stacey said. "If your food is crap, you won't get the results, and basically you are not fueling the machine to work to its potential."

Let's talk about food, then.

## eat healthy

*Came from a plant, eat it; was made in a plant, don't.*

— Michael Pollan

"I gotta start drinking unsweet tea," said the girl at the fast-food counter. "I gotta get my life together."

I had ordered an unsweet tea, and the two of us had a quick chat as she handed me my cup. She told me she was currently drinking fruit punch and a sports drink.

"And you start out feeling good and then you plummet, right?" I asked.

"I don't ever feel good," she replied.

I told the girl that when I switched from sweet tea (down South it is a serum of goodness) to unsweet, I had to ease into it. I started with half sweet, half unsweet and eventually got to where all I need is a splash of sweet to drink my tea. "Mostly unsweet with just a little sweet" is how I describe it when ordering at a restaurant. And that small change in my diet has saved me hundreds of daily calories. I love my caffeine, but I don't want diabetes.

My little conversation with that young lady was eye-opening. She recognized what is so easy to overlook: small changes make the difference. Stay small and consistent, and you can stick with it. It's like giving up sweets for Lent: one simple act can impact your routine immensely. An overnight revamp of your entire life might be fun, but it will be difficult to maintain. In fact, studies show that if you change too many things at one time, it will be almost impossible to stay the course.

Instead, start with simple choices, like parking farther out in a parking lot to get more steps in, or not finishing all the leftover desserts you find on the kids' plates. This will go a long way toward a healthy mentality and a lifestyle of good eating instead of dieting.

In a busy life — the abundant life! — healthy personal choices can be very easy to forget. One minute you are doing all the right things for body, mind, and soul, and the next you are shoveling extra handfuls of barbecue potato chips into your mouth while you make lunches.

Small choices make it easy to take care of yourself while taking care of everyone else too. Training for a marathon might be out of the question right now, but putting your health on your radar doesn't have to be.

One year I gave up sweets for Lent, and within the first week it was clear that I had a habit of grabbing a small square of dark chocolate every time I went into the pantry. How did I discover this? Because my hand reflexively ascended to that shelf whenever I went in there for something else. Whoa! I had no idea, until I was making a small, conscious decision not to eat candy. But dark chocolate isn't candy — it's good for me! True, but maybe not five and six times a day (don't tell anyone I told you that).

In a similar vein, I love red wine. It's also good for you. But in an effort to save money, I bought one of those boxes of wine, which are actually pretty tasty. The problems set in when (1) I couldn't see how much was left in the box, so I had no sense of my vino intake, and (2) it became very, very easy for me to amble into the pantry and get a splash here and there. Wanting to celebrate? Decant a little wine. Kids driving you nuts? Head to the box. I remember one early evening, two of the boys started some kind of squabble, and before I knew what I was doing I said, "Hold that thought, guys," and turned the nozzle. That's when I realized that having wine at the ready was not going to work for me, personally.

When we see how quickly we fall into bad habits, we only need a little effort to replace those with good habits. Not eating sweets can become a habit. Not eating in between meals can become a habit. And when we make small efforts in our personal goals, we will see success.

Several years ago, a summertime friend showed up at the pool at least thirty pounds lighter than the year before. I asked her what epic work she had been doing during the school year. "Not much," was her reply. At the new year, her resolution had been to eat more fruits and vegetables. So she put a bowl of produce on the dining room table and got in the habit of grabbing something from it at least once a day. Little by little, that one act — going for fruits and vegetables instead of processed snacks — led to losing a pound, and then another, and soon she found herself running in the evenings and revamping her family's lifestyle.

It can be overwhelming to think about losing ten pounds, especially with all the other things going on in life. But making a small tweak can get you moving in the right direction. The small habit of eating right makes weight control one less attention-demanding issue and something that is working in a natural, peaceful way.

Feeling good about your body, having energy, not having to make dieting a long-term, never-ending part of your life — all of this brings the peace we need to live a happy, well-ordered life.

chapter 5

# have peace in your mind

*Peace is not only desirable, but "it is the gift of God." The peace to which I am referring is not just a temporary tranquility. It is an abiding deep happiness and spiritual contentment.*

— John Taylor

W hen we take care of the body God has given us, we find peace. When we attend to how we are fueling our body and mindfully caring for our heart and lungs and muscles, we are moving in the direction of a well-ordered life. God made our mental health to be tied to our physical health. It's a cycle that's beautiful if in good working order, but vicious if off-balance.

In addition to the physical aspects of keeping our mental state healthy, there are ways of thinking and relating that impact us tremendously. These simple steps toward a well-ordered mind bring simplicity and order to our day-to-day life.

# be not afraid

*Courage, dear heart.*

— C. S. Lewis

Walking through life full of fear is exhausting. We've all been there. In my early twenties, before I had any children of my own, I was very fearful about something happening to my parents and brothers and sisters. Around the time I got married, my siblings started going to college and making life choices, and I worried so much for them in that season. Living at that level pretty much sucks the life right out of you.

Once I started having kids, there were so many opportunities to be afraid. Oh, these little babies I love so much, let me consider all the ways things can go wrong!

Once again, not the healthiest way to live.

If we aren't careful, there are countless opportunities to be afraid. As a mother, I have found that I need to be very diligent in my efforts against fear, because my "mother's intuition" can be confused with fear. We are smart people with common sense who can read a newspaper article and put two and two together; before you know it, there is a very good and compelling reason why our children should never leave our side.

I remember when Paul came home one evening after a Boy Scout meeting with our oldest son. The two of them walked in, excited to tell me all about summer Scout camp, where it would be and how long it would run. Out at the lake for a whole week — it was going to be wonderful!

"Sounds fun," I told Paul privately. "Too bad he isn't going."

"Why not?" was Paul's reply.

"Of course we aren't sending our precious twelve-year-old son to Scout camp, away from us for a whole week at the lake, where 1.2 million things can go wrong! Are you crazy? I haven't worked this hard to guide, protect, provide for, and shelter this child to have him go off and have something horrible happen at camp!"

My husband is a smart and patient man. He knew that making me feel silly or stupid or defensive was not the solution to what I would later realize was abject paranoia. He was gentle and reasonable.

"If we aren't going to move forward on this, there's no point in him continuing Scouting," said Paul. I asked him what he meant. He explained that as Ethan got older and moved closer to preparing for Eagle Scout, these kinds of opportunities would be an important part of the journey.

For the first time I stopped long enough to logically consider why Ethan shouldn't go to camp. And the answer was fear. My fear was trying to keep him from going. And my fear was masquerading as "wisdom" and "my gut" and about a thousand other words trying to make it sound more impressive.

I had to shut down the fear.

Once you allow fear into your heart as some kind of compass for making decisions or dictating emotions, you are stuck.

I've learned about myself that fear is going to always try to be a reasoned source of decision making — in my brain, in particular. That's how it's going to be, and I deal with this fear by acknowledging it and then stepping over it. We have to look fear in the eye and say, "I acknowledge your presence, but you are not allowed to have a say in this conversation."

That weird but strangely effective idea was introduced to me in a book about creativity, but I found it to be life-changing in so many areas. We can't wish away certain emotions or reactions, but we can decide that they won't run our lives. And sooner or later, the more we acknowledge and then ignore these feelings, the less sway they have in our decision making.

When you think about it, fear is reasonable and rational. But there's also a part of it that is tantamount to saying, "God doesn't care about me." When we run around being fearful all the time about all things, it's like we're living an existence outside of God and his protection. Yes, bad things happen, but we have to trust that we are on God's radar, and that we are in the center of his plan for us.

Some days it's easier to say this than others. But this is always the truth.

"We can feel that growing in love should make life 'easier,'" writes Sister Wendy Beckett, "that there is some failure in our fear, temptation, struggle. Not so. In fact the tempest may blow more severely as we near harbor. Jesus could never know a psychic respite, as the Gospels show. But our *attitudes* change. We cease to be afraid of fear; we open our arms to the will for the Father to give us whatever he will, *knowing*, in Jesus, that he gives only 'good things'" (*Spiritual Letters*).

Anthony de Mello, in *Selected Writings*, says this:

> Has it ever struck you that those who most fear to die are the ones who most fear to live? Life is flexible and free, and you are rigid and frozen. Life carries all things away, and you crave stability and permanence. You fear life and death because you cling. You cannot bear the thought of losing a relative or friend; you dread losing a pet theory or ideology or belief. When you cling to nothing, when you have no fear of losing anything, then you are free to flow like a mountain stream that is always fresh and sparkling and alive.

We can experience freedom when we learn to let go, to offer to God all the things we are afraid might happen. We find peace and order in admitting that our anxiety and fears do not keep our loved ones safe — and that they are not what keep us safe. We slowly learn to trust God in each of these areas of our life, from our safety and our children's safety, even down to our very existence and acceptance. We know that God cares for us and will take care of us, that he will give us everything we need.

What a simple, beautiful concept to live by.

# go out with (good) friends

*Faithful friends are a sturdy shelter;*
*whoever finds one finds a treasure.*
*Faithful friends are beyond price,*
*no amount can balance their worth.*
*Faithful friends are life-saving medicine;*
*those who fear God will find them.*
— Sirach 6:14–16

Isolation is one of the biggest obstacles to mental health. Even Mother Teresa noted the importance of feeling connected and included.

"Loneliness and the feeling of being unwanted is the most terrible poverty," she said.

I'm a weird mix of introvert/extrovert. Maybe we all are to some degree. I handle stress and feeling overwhelmed by making sure I get the quiet time I need. I can handle being around people — I love it, in fact — but only when I have a good balance of those chunks of time that involve me being quiet. This is hard to come by in some seasons, and if I say yes to too many things, and don't get the settled feeling and ability to slow down and be quiet, I struggle. Anxiety creeps in when my brain doesn't have time to process, reflect, and be still.

But for people like me, people who are very outgoing and equally energized by time alone, we run the risk of isolating ourselves if we aren't careful. And while I often think that I don't need a "girls' night out" or to make plans with friends, I find that if I go too long without being around others, I start to lose my sense of perspective.

As we get older, I think we can all admit that our circle of trusted friends shrinks, or at the very least doesn't continue to expand. I don't think this is because we are meeting fewer people, but because we learn the importance of trusted friends. Also, we're busy. Selfishly, when I actually do have a free evening, if I'm going to make an effort to be around other people, I want the time to be edifying.

There are two ways of looking at how we spend time with other people. One is the concept of hospitality, of the corporal works of mercy and being Jesus to those around us. We are willing to open our home and be real with people, and perhaps start to build something that could turn into a deeper friendship. Those gatherings are important, and we should even schedule those.

But then there are those times we need to be around people who truly "get" us, around whom we can really be ourselves. I have a group of people around whom I can let it all hang out. I can show my weakness, or ask them to pray for me, or even admit to them something stupid and embarrassing I said or did. And I know they won't judge me. They won't walk away and talk about me. All they want is the best for me, including even letting me be a not-the-very-best version of myself because maybe I'm going through a bad time.

We need those people in our life, and we can only get them through hard work, commitment, and time. We build this kind of friendship, and those women and men become like our sisters and brothers. This deep friendship involves cultivating community, knowing these people have long loved you and will continue to love you. The Church needs this kind of friendship because this is true fraternal love. We build the Church when we can be real, because in being strong enough to be vulnerable, we grow in our faith, which helps us grow in our ability to love and be loved. This kind of love can transform the world!

Also, it's fun.

Have you ever been with a group of friends who made you laugh so hard you couldn't breathe? This kind of friendship, at its most pure and fun, is transformative. Many times, I get so wrapped up in my headspace that I lose sight of reality, of the ability to calm my bad self down. And then I'll get an invite to go grab a margarita with my crew and I'll think, "No, I couldn't possibly. Who has time for such merriment? I must stay home and ponder all the ways I need to improve my home and myself and my world...." But I push through, because deep down I know it will be good for me. I always come home a totally different person, as my husband can attest. After I've laughed and been honest and gotten outside of my head, I find myself back to being that true, free version of myself. I'm happy, and I know God loves me, because I've been loved on so very much.

In these moments, we know we aren't alone. This friendship love tears down the walls that make me think I am the only person struggling with my own weird problems. And maybe you, too, struggle with your own unique problems, but you are not alone. You need to know that. You need to be told that every minute of every day, or as often as you can bear to hear it. You are not alone. You are not crazy. You are doing awesome. You are going to make it.

Invest in this kind of friendship. If you have those kinds of friends, make time for them. If you don't have those kinds of friendships, ask God to send some your way.

Making friends can be a scary, challenging endeavor. While I suggest praying that God sends you friends, there are also some practical things you can do. If you feel like you have no one in your life, try joining a mothers' group at your parish. Or you and your husband can join (or start!) a small group at your church. Invite neighbors over for dinner and see what friendships might blossom from that hospitality. As my mom often told me when I was growing up and complaining that I had no friends (which was never true), "If you want a friend, be a friend." Don't sit back and feel sorry for yourself. Go find someone who needs a friend as much as you do!

God loves us so much, and he wants us to feel supported and encouraged. He doesn't want us to be a lonely traveler on our path. We need pilgrims traveling with us, holding us up when we feel tired, and encouraging us when we are sad and disappointed.

Pride and fear would tell us that we can't possibly show who we really are, that to show our struggles and fears would make us less attractive. But the harder we try to hide our flaws, the more painful it is to relate to the world around us. You don't have to share all the things with all the people, but invest in people who know you and love you in spite of it all. When you are loved, you can love yourself. When you love yourself, you are better equipped to love the world around you.

# choose joy

*We are at Jesus' disposal. If he wants you to be sick in bed, if he wants you to proclaim his work in the street, if he wants you to clean the toilets all day, that's all right, everything is all right. We must say, "I belong to you. You can do whatever you like." And this is our strength. This is the joy of the Lord.*
— Saint Teresa of Calcutta

Choose Joy. I am always hearing that concept — such a nice idea. Choose joy! I think I will.

But if you think about it too much, it's more of a lifestyle choice than a practical directive. Yes, I'll choose joy! Where do I sign up, what does this even mean?

If the idea is too theoretical, it doesn't mean much. It's a place we will arrive at some day, or maybe even the expression we keep on our faces. Joy! See it, here's my happy mask!

In the middle of a chilly week in March, the idea came to me that to choose joy had to be an actual, well, choice. I was struggling with some negative thinking while also in the midst of a Lent that didn't seem too fruitful. My forty-day fast had started off with giving up sweets, but hormones decided that wasn't feasible. (If that sounds wimpy to you, give yourself a few years. In college, I once had a Lent that included fasting from sweets, meat, bread, Coca-Cola, and television.) I know how to fast. I can embrace the suffering.

But here I was, and Lent was kicking my rear. I couldn't even go a few hours without foraging for a few chocolate chips at the bottom of my freezer. I was desperate, and also pathetic.

In addition to that, my thought life was kind of a mess. The negative thinking was out of control, not because I enjoyed bad thoughts but because these thoughts kept creeping into my mental landscape. It was here, in the midst of my Lenten failings — eating all the sweets, thinking all the thoughts — that I had a spark of inspiration. It wasn't my idea, as much as I would love to take credit. It was divine inspiration, I think, that gently, lovingly pointed out that I should stop beating myself up for the bad thoughts and instead offer them back to Jesus.

"Give them to God," said the thought.

"What in the world would he want with these dingy rags," was my reply. My thoughts aren't anything I'm terribly proud to share with God or anyone else.

But I knew, somehow, in that moment, that my thoughts were exactly what God wanted. He wanted these split-second moments where I struggled — those thoughts that pop into my head before I had a chance to rebuke them. He was okay with this, I realized, because I could offer them back to him. You see, this kind of negativity feels like suffering to me. I don't want to have a default setting of pessimism. I don't enjoy being critical.

But my brain, I'm afraid to admit, is sometimes like water: it seeks out the lowest spot. And as my thoughts trickle forth, I am easily distracted by the thing currently agitating me the most, the low point, the nadir. Also, I'm quick to form habits, which means, if I have had a negative encounter early in the day, that thing robs me of my peace.

So there I sat at my desk, lamenting a bad Lent and ingesting sugar and the pathetic train of thoughts, and God said: "Give it. I'll take it." And there, in that moment of grace, I thought: "Okay. Let's give it a try."

So I did. I made a conscious decision to actively, and with great passion, hold every single negative thought captive for Christ: as in, the moment that thought entered my head, I acknowledged it, and then said: "Here you go, God. This is for you!"

What a weird thing, to think God wanted that. But he did, and I offered it to him. And then I did it again. And again. Because, as I've said, I'm a creature of habit, and nothing if not committed. So all of these thoughts, which I had gotten in my committed habit of allowing in, I immediately swatted up to God, like a Wimbledon player returning the serve.

And then, something amazing happened.

The thing that was offering me defeat and dejection became a bright light. These thoughts became something positive. All within a few hours. Because I had decided to bite off a small, ingestible portion — every negative thought between now and lunch — it was doable for me.

My decision to *choose joy*! wasn't about a lifetime commitment. It was about a Wednesday morning commitment. This, I could handle. This was totally doable.

Do this: Choose joy. For the next two hours, hold every thought captive. Don't aim for choosing joy for weeks on end. Do it for one day, this day. This moment. And then the next moment. Every moment between now and your next meal, but one moment at a time. Every time a negative thought creeps in, shut it down immediately. Don't give it any oxygen, don't let it fester and grow. Give the thought to God, trade it in for freedom and joy.

The negative thought becomes a gift, because it is a reminder to focus on God. It also offers the gift of humility, because it's a beautiful reminder that you aren't perfect. You need God's grace.

For me, I saw an immediate change in my outlook. Within an hour of doing this, my spirit had lifted. Within a few hours, my day had turned around. This decision to choose joy was a small to-do, not a grand, life-changing decision. It was a small step, without me even thinking about the larger issues.

In this moment, right now, I choose joy. And tomorrow, I'll do it again.

# get over yourself, be imperfect

*She could never be a saint, but she thought*
*she could be a martyr if they killed her quick.*
— Flannery O'Connor (from "A Temple of the Holy Ghost")

I'm one of those people who likes to replay conversations in my mind. For too many years, if I went out with friends or to a party with Paul, I would wake up in the night and think over all the things I said. I would replay the sound of my voice, and then chide myself for how obnoxious I certainly looked and sounded. I worried I had sounded too prideful or gossipy, or that I had talked too loud or too much. I had a hunch everyone else was also at home awake in the middle of the night thinking all the same thoughts (about me!).

One time, I had a conversation about this with a friend, who told me to stop apologizing for yet another thing I worried I had said. "You realize, no one is thinking about all the things YOU said," she told me. "They are busy worrying about themselves!"

It's probably a form of pride to think that when we mess up, it's some big shocking thing. But being human is a big part of, well, being human. We are flawed, sinful beings — and thank you, Lord, for your saving grace and love. If God can love me unconditionally, perhaps I can learn to extend some of that same kindness to myself.

Embracing our imperfections needs to happen on so many levels. I'm a sinner; I'm not always perfect. That's taking the concept to its core. But we also need to welcome that same "imperfection" into the various areas of our lives — motherhood, especially. I think it's hard not being a perfect mother, in part, because we take the vocation of motherhood so seriously. We recognize family life as a gift — a call! — from God, and we want to give it the time and energy it deserves.

But trying to equate doing a good job with perfection will only make you crazy.

I'll never forget the day I sort of caught on that life with a pack of boys meant motherhood was not going to look like anything I had predicted. I was struggling, really struggling, with being a mama to so many little boys. And I had a moment of grace when I realized I had to love the imperfections of the situation or I would go nuts.

So I started embracing the craziness of life with boys, learning to laugh at the insane things they did while also gently redirecting them toward sanity and obedience. I also started to see what a gift this "imperfection" was in my life. Very early on in my mothering gig, I had to drop the charade of having my act together. Little boys have a way of helping you realize and admit that you are not fooling anyone, most especially yourself.

Loving our weakness, getting over ourselves, is one of the surest steps on the path of sanity, peace, joy, and simplicity. We aren't carrying the weight of a "false life," as Saint John Paul II said, and we move closer to that true freedom that comes with laughing at our flaws because we know we are forgiven and loved by a mighty Savior.

This beautiful quote from the Holy Father addressing World Youth Day 2000 always inspires me to focus on true perfection, and not on the emptiness of trying to impress those around me. He said:

> It is Jesus in fact that you seek when you dream of happiness; he is waiting for you when nothing else you find satisfies you; he is the beauty to which you are so attracted; it is he who provokes you with that thirst for fullness that will not let you settle for compromise; it is he who urges you to shed the masks of a false life; it is he who reads in your hearts your most genuine choices, the choices that others try to stifle. It is Jesus who stirs in you the desire to do something great with your lives, the will to follow an ideal, the refusal to allow yourselves to be grounded down by mediocrity, the courage to commit yourselves humbly and patiently to

improving yourselves and society, making the world more human and more fraternal.

Let go of the ideals you have in motherhood, in family life, in being a human. Try your very best. Pray for grace. Pursue heroic virtue. And ask God to show you all the ways he loves when you don't always get everything right.

# dine alone

*The world is upside down because there is so very little love in the home. We have no time for our children; we have no time for each other; and there is no time to enjoy each other. That is why there is so much suffering and so much unhappiness in the world today. Everybody seems to be in such a terrible rush, anxious for what is bigger and better and greater, and mothers and fathers often do not have time for each other, let alone their children. In the home begins the disruption of the peace of the world.*

— Saint Teresa of Calcutta, *No Greater Love*

This next section is about how dining alone will make you feel less lonely. Weird but true.

I am a huge fan of dining alone. It's so strange to me that not everyone does this regularly! Maybe it's because I have this three-fold love of (1) unsweet tea with a little sweet, (2) making lists, and (3) writing in restaurants. Sitting at a table getting refills and writing is my happy place. I consider it to be the ultimate in self-care.

Dining alone is an important part of simplifying your life because it's a chance to slow down and think. You aren't at home, where it's tempting to take bites of a boring old sandwich while you unload the dishwasher and wipe down the counters. You're away from the tasks of home life, able to sit and settle and think.

I rarely bring a book with me, but that's another excellent idea. I tend to use this time to think about my week, what I have coming up that needs my attention, and what I need to be getting ready for. I usually start some kind of list that has two columns: "To Do" and "To Buy." Once I get going, I add a third section: "Groceries." Usually on the back of that piece of paper I start my weekly menu. If I'm getting the job done, I will have brought my weekly calendar with me, to cross-check the events of the week and what we can realistically have to eat on each of those nights (grilling, for instance, is not a great choice for evenings when you walk in the door at 7:30).

Are you starting to believe me when I say dining alone is an important part of a simplified life? It gives you time to think and to plan. It's a chance to get your ducks in a row, to prepare to go home and love your family. Sitting in the stillness of your own pace with your own food — contemplating, musing, formulating, dreaming. I sit and do all of these things, and when I leave I'm ready to take on the world — to go out and care for my people because I've taken a few minutes to care for myself.

Also, one of the things I enjoy about dining alone is that I get to choose exactly where I want to go, where I want to sit, and how long I want to take to eat. Dining alone means I don't have to worry that I'm the world's slowest eater and that I don't like to talk and eat at the same time. It's so great!

Of course, I realize that one of the reasons I enjoy dining alone is that I am rarely alone. If I'm eating by myself, even once or twice a week, it's generally my only solitude. So I enjoy the luxury of this time.

But more than that, dining alone helps me slow down and take stock. I can refuel and get organized. And also, it's a lot of fun. And afterward, I climb back into my van, head back to my people, and get back to the business of running my household.

chapter 6

# have peace in your spirit and heart

*Be very careful to retain peace of heart, because Satan casts his lines in troubled waters.*

— St Paul of the Cross

We have talked about taking care of your body and caring for your mind. Now we're going to address caring for your spirit.

What is your spirit? John 4:23–24 describes the spirit as the part of each of us that connects with God:

> "But the hour is coming, and is now here, when true worshipers will worship the Father in Spirit and truth; and indeed the Father seeks such people to worship him. God is Spirit, and those who worship him must worship in Spirit and truth."

According to the *Catechism of the Catholic Church*, "the human person, created in the image of God, is a being at once corporeal and spiritual" (CCC 362), and "'Spirit' signifies that from creation":

man is ordered to a supernatural end and that his soul can gratuitously be raised beyond all it deserves to communion with God.

The spiritual tradition of the Church also emphasizes the *heart*, in the biblical sense of the depths of one's being, where the person decides for or against God. (CCC 367-368, emphasis in original)

So we need and want peace in our spirit and heart. We need to simplify within us that space that searches for God, that wants unity with him.

An important part of finding peace in our spirit is knowing, at the very core of our being, how much we are loved by our Creator. That knowledge and experience of this love gives us peace. We cut through all the junk of being separated from God, the things that keep us away from him (sin, our temptations, our wounds, our opinions), so that we are moving freely and without these burdens. We begin to trust not only that he cares for us, but that he has a great plan for us.

"For I know well the plans I have in mind for you — oracle of the LORD — plans for your welfare and not for woe, so as to give you a future of hope" (Jeremiah 29:11).

## love yourself — be a saint

*Be who God meant you to be and you will set the world on fire.*
— Saint Catherine of Siena

I have this memory of being at a giant youth conference. I was a junior in high school, and thousands of us teenagers were standing in a tent in the middle of a field at a Catholic college campus. We had been singing and praying, and then the speaker asked us all if we wanted to be saints. In that moment, I remember looking around and yelling "Nooooo!" at the top of my lungs, arms in air, only to look around in shock as everyone around me was yelling "Yesssss!" Two of my friends were behind me. Their expressions upon seeing me rebuke the offer to be a saint, as they themselves were agreeing to it, made me realize I had given the wrong answer.

I was thinking about saints, but only about the martyrs. That's what I thought the speaker was asking. Heck no did I want to be a martyr! Eventually, I realized that the question was not if we wanted to be tied to a tree and shot at with arrows. I was asked if I wanted to be holy.

Do I want to be holy? Ohhhhh, yesssss!

But even if the answer is yes, that doesn't mean it's easy. The idea of being a saint seems so overwhelming and out of reach. Growing up, all the stories I had ever read about saints made them seem like some superior life-form destined for holiness.

But then I met a saint. And I began to realize that the saints are amazing, radical, and just like us.

One summer in college I met Mother Teresa. I was serving with her sisters in the Bronx, and she came to town to receive an award from the Knights of Columbus. She came to the chapel where my fellow volunteers went to Mass each day, and I got to sit right by her during Mass. She was so tiny and unassuming, I didn't even realize it was her! I was looking for someone giant and larger-than-life.

Later that day, the camp volunteers all got to meet her, and she gave us each a miraculous medal. She spent some time talking to us, a very simple message of remembering that everything we do, we do for Jesus.

"You did it for me," she said, holding up one finger for each word. This is what Jesus tells us; this is what we have to remember.

And that's what the saints do. They do it for Jesus. Whatever it is Jesus asks of them, they do. And that's what makes sainthood possible for us too.

The saints were all different. For me, I spent so many years feeling that God messed up when he made me. I had decided as a teenager that someone with my loud, kinda bossy, kinda nosy personality was not the saintly type. The saints all seemed

so quiet and perfect, not people who struggled with real problems like the rest of us. My very best friend since I was four
was one of those people who always kept her mouth shut and
her opinions to herself (at least in group settings), who didn't
talk too much, and who remembered to spend time in prayer
every evening. She could be a saint, I always thought, but I
didn't see myself as one of the elect.

And then, years later, I picked up a book on personal holiness, *Fire Within*, by Father Thomas Dubay, S.M. Within the
first fifteen pages, Father Dubay introduced me to Saint Teresa
of Ávila, whom I only ever knew as a doctor of the Church
(and thus, perfect).

Teresa, it turns out, was known for her "excessive chattiness," and in that second I felt like I had come home.

"Yet Teresa had her faults," writes Father Dubay, "for saints
are not born out of the blue. They are weighed down with the
same weak human nature we all have, and they experience the
same temptations. The difference is that they say a complete Yes
to the healing grace God offers to everyone, whereas most of us
say 'maybe,' or 'somewhat' or 'wait a while ... not yet.'"

Reading those words opened up a whole new world. I
might not ever be canonized, I thought, but I could pursue
being a saint, whatever that meant.

What it meant was learning to find God in the center of
everything I did, and to see everything I did as what God
wanted of me in that moment. Folding this load of laundry,
driving this carpool, feeding this hungry, cranky child. These
were the things God asked of me, and I would do them for
him. I would give him my YES in each moment, as often as I
could remember. In doing so, Jesus could act in me and I could
grow in love for him. If I moved about the hours of my day
with a trust that whatever I was doing was what God wanted
me to be doing, I would have incredible peace.

In *Searching for and Maintaining Peace*, Father Jacques Philippe
compares the fruit of this peace — allowing God's grace to act
in us throughout our day — to the surface of a lake:

If the surface of the lake is peaceful and tranquil, the sun will be reflected in this lake; and the more peaceful the lake, the more perfectly will it be reflected. If, on the contrary, the surface of the lake is agitated, undulating, then the image of the sun cannot be reflected in it. It is a little bit like this with regard to our soul in relationship to God. The more our soul is peaceful and tranquil, the more God is reflected in it, the more His image expresses itself in us, the more His grace acts through us. On the other hand, if our soul is agitated and troubled, the grace of God is able to act only with much greater difficulty.

We reflect the beauty and glory of God when we do what he asks of us, and when we do it for him. We radiate peace because we trust that whatever we are doing is what God wants us to be doing, which means it will draw us closer to him.

But this trust also must reach us at our core. It's not merely finding God in the act of what we are doing — it's finding him in who we are. Who I am, this person, me with my "excessive chattiness" — I am fearfully and wonderfully made! God made me and he loves me.

This is the heart of being a saint: to do what God needs us to do, and to be who he made us to be! We need to love who we are, knowing that if we are pursuing holiness, God will help burn away the parts of us that are out of order. Holiness is a life of total devotion to God — every part of my life, my being, and my actions are devoted to God. That includes what I do, and also who I am.

There is so much freedom and peace when we learn to love who we are, knowing that God made us and that we are his. Love yourself!

In fact, celebrate who you are! The person you are is exactly who God made you to be. And being yourself, this amazing person God made, will put you on the path to sainthood, to sanctification.

I was working at a fund-raising yard sale for my son Charlie's senior class when I came across an old, wrinkled, worn-out-from-reading pamphlet, "How to be a Saint." It is a quick, life-changing read:

> It is a great thing to realise that in order to be saints we have only to be what God made us to be, and to do what God made us to do. If we are clever, then to be clever; if not clever, then not to be clever; if we are successful, then to be successful; if not successful, then not to be successful; if in good health, then to be healthy; if sickly, then to be sickly; and so on. Perfect simplicity with regard to ourselves; perfect contentment with everything that comes our way, perfect peace of mind in utter self-forgetfulness. This becomes easier the more we realise the utter greatness and goodness and allness of God. That last ingredient consists in fixing our attention on God in our meditations, and in cultivating a sense of proportion. Then we realise our own utter insignificance and worthlessness and nothingness. If we see the whole we shall easily despise the trifles; if we lose ourselves in God how puny the rest appears!
>
> This is the cure for making too much of little things, whether they go right or whether they go wrong, which is the cause of all our loss of peace of mind. This is the real test of sanctity, that simplicity of trust in God which is the perfection of human nature. In the end, when life is done and all is over, such a soul is found more precious than one who has shone in many deeds.
>
> Therefore let us make a great deal of God[,] forgetting if we can at times everything else in His presence.
>
> Let us make nothing at all of ourselves, whether we are clever, or whether we are not, whether we are loved or whether we are not, whether we succeed or

whether we do not, whether we get what we desire or do not.

In the midst of all we can rejoice that we are what He has made us, that those things happen which He wants to happen, that if all the world were to collapse and the very Heavens were to fall, there would still be the great living, loving God. That should be a very consoling thought for those who are in danger: to think that although all about them may be shaking and falling to the ground, God does not shake, God is solid, the one stable thing, and we can live on that stability no matter if the whole world is rocking about us. God is not moved, God is not beaten.

So, if we want to be saints, let us sit still often in the presence of God, lost in acts of faith, and love and hope, in acts of praise, and adoration and thanksgiving.

When the thought of ourselves and our own petty worries creeps in, let us sit still again in His presence, with acts of humility and contrition, and oblation, telling Him how small we are, how sorry we are for ourselves, how we would like to be and do better.

When the human heart is hungry as at times it must be, come again to the feet of God, and fill it with acts of longing for Him and His love and glory, rather than with the little husks of self-satisfaction; fill it with acts of rejoicing in Him and in His tremendous almightiness, such that nothing in the world matters anything at all.

Let us pray like this and we shall lay the foundation on which sanctity is built; live like this and sanctity will build itself; let us die like this and we shall die good and faithful servants. (Orphans Press Rodale)

# love your life

*The two most important days in your life are the day you are born
and the day you find out why.*

— Mark Twain

The first step in loving your life is recognizing that it's a vocation — a sacred call from God that is part of your sanctification. Your being a wife and mom is what is helping you get
to heaven! Thank the Lord when you wake up. Your life is a
divine mission and call.

It's dangerous to get the idea that life is passing us by. This
is especially easy when we have small children, and daily life
is enough of a challenge. It's amazing how much babies and
toddlers can dictate our activities and schedules.

A few years ago I was invited to visit Santa Ana, El Sal-
vador, and write about the charitable sponsorship program
called Unbound. I went with a group of fellow writers, and
we got to meet the men, women, and children whose lives
were positively impacted by a thirty-dollar monthly commitment. It was beautiful and life-changing. And while I missed
my husband and children back home, I loved the power of
sharing what I saw, in the hope of increasing sponsors, to get
help for more needy children and elderly. One afternoon, we
drove up into the mountains on the outskirts of town. We saw
how people lived off the land and picked coffee in wild forests.
That afternoon, I rode down the mountain in the back of a
truck filled with other volunteers and workers, and off in the
distance was a volcano — a real, live volcano! — and life felt
glorious and amazing!

Fast-forward forty-eight or ninety-six hours, and I found
myself back home, standing in front of my washing machine,
sorting clothes. I was hunched over my front loader, turning
a black, crusty basketball sock right-side out, and I said to the
Lord, "This is not the best use of my gifts."

The words sort of hung in the air for a minute, this thing I
said to God, about me and my fabulous gifts and how I could be

changing the world right in that moment if only I wasn't stuck here doing this lame chore. And what I heard back from God was not so much a correction or a reprimand but a warmth, a smile almost. And I felt peace, like God was reminding me that what I was doing in that exact moment was indeed the best use of my time, because it was the thing God wanted me to be doing. Freedom comes from knowing we are where we need to be, and if we aren't exactly where we should be, God is with us on our journey closer to that spot.

Catherine Doherty writes about the Duty of the Moment, and learning to embrace it:

> The duty of the moment is what you should be doing at any given time, in whatever place God has put you. If you have a child, your duty of the moment may be to change a dirty diaper. So you do it. But you don't just change that diaper, you change it to the best of your ability, with great love for both God and the child. Do you do it that way? You can see Christ in that child....
>
> Your doing the duty of the moment, your living the nitty-gritty, daily routine of ordinary life, can uncover the face of Christ in the marketplace. Christ can come into the place where you work or play or eat. He will come into your home or into a restaurant. He will come into a school or a company cafeteria or a subway or wherever.... So this is what I mean. You, as a Christian, as a follow of Christ, do your duty of the moment. Whatever your duty is, you do it with great love. And as you do, the image of Christ, the icon of Christ, will be shown to people wherever you are — in your home, in your place of work outside the home, in your school, in the neighborhood where you live, in your church, in the grocery store, wherever you happen to be. ("The Duty of the Moment," *Dear Parents: A Gift of Love for Families*)

For me, I can only love my life with abandon when I trust that God knows me and loves me and has me doing what he needs me to do. If what we are doing right now is what God needs us to do, it's the thing drawing us closer to being a saint.

You are traveling toward sainthood! What better adventure could there possibly be?

Of course, some days will be better than others. But praise God in the highs and in the lows. And trust in his great love for you.

We learn to love our life when we cling to that truth: God has you doing this for such a time as this. These people for you to love. This home for you to care for. This husband. These children. This is your mission. Don't look around to see how it compares to everybody else's.

"Comparison is the thief of joy," said Theodore Roosevelt. Isn't that the truth. How many times have I been perfectly content with my own little world, my own children, until I see what someone else is up to? Talk about an instant buzz kill. If we want peace, we have to focus on the joy and fulfillment of the life we are living, not another's life.

When we compare, we are judging our interior against someone else's exterior. We are taking the areas where we fail and putting them up against an area where someone else succeeds. What a recipe for disaster! Of course, we walk away feeling like a loser; it's a natural result.

I spent years watching better-behaved children sit through Mass while my sons begged and pleaded to leave, or heaved a shoulder into their neighboring brother. I felt like a complete failure as a mother and as a Catholic. I spent my time at Mass switching between trying to keep my children in line and envying every other family that wasn't in the same boat as me. It was a painful time.

But what about the people who seem to have it all together at Mass? They've got other things they're dealing with. And even if they don't, that's okay. God gave you these children, this husband, this life. Thank him for that, and pray for the wisdom to train your kids the way they should go. Love your children and train them, but also embrace who they are. They are a gift from God!

When you look at someone else, be inspired. But don't go beyond that. Love your life and be so committed to it that when you get up each morning the devil says, "Oh, no! She's up!" There is so much power in loving who we are and the life God's given us!

And in the midst of this, don't forget the practical part of peace: doing the things that bring us peace. Pursuing order in our home, finding peace within ourselves, and taking care of those areas that need our attention bring us peace, which helps us love our life even more. Be determined to love your life, which also means being willing to address the parts of it that can be changed.

# unplug

*I went to the woods because I wished to live deliberately, to front only the essential facts of life, and see if I could not learn what it had to teach, and not, when I came to die, discover that I had not lived.*
— Henry David Thoreau, *Walden*

Continuing on the theme of having peace in your spirit and your heart, and also avoiding the comparison trap — step away from your phone! Step away from social media! Take some time to really focus on your own life and world, and the beautiful, wonderful adventure you are experiencing.

We live in an amazing time in regards to technology, but that same tech also opens windows and doors that can be a challenge. We are privy to information like never before. I love that no matter what question my children ask, I'm able to quickly and easily find the answer. How amazing!

But that practical knowledge isn't all we have access to. We also get to see what our neighbor had for lunch yesterday and all of the end-of-the-school-year awards your second cousin once removed's kid received.

Yes, we are happy for those people, like those people are happy for us in our shining moments. But it can become a little overwhelming at times, keeping up with the Joneses and the Joneses' neighbors and cousins and in-laws. Also, I've found that I'm on social media the most when I'm tired, unmotivated, and picking up my phone to buy some time. That's not a great state of mind to be in when I start looking at what people are sharing. Plus, what people are sharing tends to be the highs of their life. When you look up and see your own reality (laundry, kids squabbling, bills to pay), the contrast can be exhausting.

Now, this isn't sour grapes! In general, I enjoy seeing pictures and keeping up with information. But it's not for everyone, and it's definitely not for all the time. We need to have limits. I read one suggestion that we get in the habit of "fasting" from technology one hour a day, one day a week, one week a year. I'm not sure how feasible that is (having teenage drivers means I always need to be available), but giving yourself a break from being constantly "plugged in" is a relief.

I'm also embarrassed to admit that once I start "checking" things on my phone it becomes a reflexive nonstop habit. Check, check, check — like my life depends on it.

I'm learning to set limits, not because I have times when social media doesn't bring out the best in me but because it's a distraction.

Be present.

Get unplugged.

Look up and see the world around you, not the world in that tiny glass screen. Connect with nature! Hear, see, feel, BE!

Live your own life. Recognize Jesus in the center of what you are doing, and focus on his call to you. That's where the sense of adventure and joy comes from.

Thank you, God, for what you are asking of me today! Thank you for your beautiful creation, for the actual world around and in front of me.

part III

# peace and order in our spiritual growth: Jesus, others, you

*Accepting oneself does not preclude an attempt to become better.*
— Flannery O'Connor

This last section of the book is the heart of it all — the spiritual life. It's taking all of the practical of the first part of the book, ordering home and self, and allowing that order and peace to draw us closer to Jesus.

In our relationship with God, there are three approaches, or pathways, that help us grow in holiness:

- There is our relationship with Jesus, the time we spend with him in pure friendship.
- There are our relationships with others, the people God puts in our path. Those are opportunities not

simply to love God's people but also to grow in holiness and virtue through our interactions with others.

- And finally, there is you. You are the connecting factor between the end of this circle (the spiritual life and your relationship with God) and the beginning (the peace and order you are striving for in your home and in your person).

Order in your home contributes to order within you (mentally, emotionally), which leads to a greater ability to have order in the spiritual life. And an ordered spiritual life definitely lends itself to order in your practical life. And there the healthy cycle feeds itself.

So let's talk about spirituality. Jesus. Others. You. What a wonderful way to spell JOY!

chapter 7

# spirituality and Jesus

*A rule I have had for years is to treat the Lord Jesus Christ
as a personal friend. It is not a creed, a mere empty doctrine,
but it is Christ himself we have.*

— D. L. Moody

Of course, Jesus is at the heart of our spiritual lives (this
is where I'm tempted to say "Duh," but this part of the
book feels more serious, so I won't). Jesus and spirituality is a
no-brainer; yet our lives are filled with so many distractions
that we often forget that he is the heart, the absolute, most
basic part of the Christian walk. There are prayers and pil-
grimages and purifications, so many ways to get closer to God.
But at the heart of every single tool we use to grow, it's Jesus
that we seek.

## spend time in prayer

*Contemplative prayer ... in my opinion is nothing else than a close sharing between friends; it means taking time frequently to be alone with him who we know loves us.*

— Saint Teresa of Ávila

The greatest gift you can give yourself in the spiritual life is learning to make it personal. It's important to recognize and proclaim your love for Jesus. It's equally, if not more important, for you to embrace his love for you. That love heals and comforts and clarifies. It brings wisdom and joy and puts everything else in perspective. God's love for you gives you grace and peace, and it helps you make sense of your life, worth, and existence in this space and time. It is your sanity.

We can say grand, glorious, theoretical things. But if it doesn't feel personal, what's the point?

Now, I'm not saying the spiritual experience needs to be some giant ball of emotion. Some people enjoy the mountaintop experience (I sure do!). But that's not the point of spirituality. In fact, the real growth comes from those seasons where God doesn't necessarily feel very close, but we still embrace his peace and joy.

But God's plan for us isn't that he would always feel far from us. He wants us to know that he is with us. In order to get in the habit of knowing this, we have to spend time with him. In the same way as friendship grows when two people spend time together, so our relationship with God is built and strengthened when we spend time with him.

Once upon a time, I thought spending time in prayer was about quantity. I got a little tripped up with this because I was a mom with lots of little kids, and I was shooting for some kind of one-hour-a-day prayer time that involved lots of Scripture reading and very long prayer lists. I'm sorry to admit, that sounds like an absolute chore to me now, not only because it felt like a research project (who else does God need me to tell him about?) but also because quiet time was almost unheard of. No matter how early I got up in those years, if I was awake in the house, the boys could tell. They would get up and find me, and there was the end of that hour. I also struggled with the fact that while I was theoretically sitting around telling God about all my problems, the laundry wasn't getting folded and the kitchen wasn't being cleaned.

Looking back now, I can see that I had it all wrong. God doesn't desire a sense of obligation. He doesn't have an ideal prayer time that only counts if we get it right. He is here for me because he loves me and wants to spend time with me.

And then one day I discovered I have the strongest sense of God's presence in my laundry room. When I'm tucked away in this quiet spot, folding warm, fresh-smelling clothes right out of the dryer, I feel God. I know he is there. I feel his love.

So that has become my prayer time. And I don't mean I stand there telling God how to fix my problems. Somehow in feeling his love for me, I don't worry so much about telling him what to fix. I have this sense that he knows. Sure, I offer up my cares and concerns to him. But for me, my prayer time has become simply experiencing God's love. I stand there and fold clothes and accept God's love for me. He is with me there, and as I move throughout my day.

It's simple. It's easy. It's totally transformative.

But I do want to address the importance of spiritual reading and sitting still. It's not enough to say, "My life is a prayer!" People who are working to get in good shape aren't content with saying their life is a workout video. You work on the things you want. And so, spending time in the quiet, with an active focus on God, is good. We find God in the folding of laundry, and we also grow closer to him through Scripture study and spiritual reading. The two need to work together.

# have peace with God, learn to trust

*How can anyone benefit and share his gifts lavishly if he doesn't understand that he is rich? In my opinion it is impossible because of our nature for someone who doesn't know he is favored by God to have enthusiasm for great things.*

— Saint Teresa of Ávila

Once upon a time, a few years ago, I had the most stressful experience in Eucharistic Adoration. There I sat, trying to connect with God. All I could do was look at the people around me and worry about where I "ranked." What could I possibly bring to God that someone else wasn't already bringing? "I bet that lady three rows up has way more to offer than me." I sat and fretted and felt so utterly aware of my own worthlessness, my unworthiness.

There was a hole, a fear within me, that I could never compare to all the other men and women also trying to be holy.

And the truth is, I can't. I won't. I never will. I'm a sinner and that's that. What a relief to get that out there.

Sitting there in the Adoration chapel wasn't about where I ranked in the list of those people. Life isn't a competition! The spiritual life definitely isn't a competition. Pursuing holiness isn't about seeing who gets farther on the board, who has traveled enough spaces on "overcoming venial sins" and is moving toward that winning space called "Sainthood!"

We are all sinners. We are all broken.

What God was doing that day with each of those people in the Adoration chapel was unique, beautiful, and very, very personal. It's not some ordered list with all of us trying to figure out where we are ranked.

I remember sharing this with my spiritual adviser and him explaining to me that what we bring — what I bring — is simply the thing within my soul that only I have to offer. The thing I can bring to Jesus is simply me. No one else has me — Rachel — to offer Jesus. And the same is true for you. Hooray! There is no competition here; it is simply me and myself and the simple, humble gift of offering myself to God.

This is the ultimate act of trusting God, of spirituality and Jesus. It is recognizing that I only have myself to offer — and for God, that is enough.

In the silence, I offer myself to God. In the silence, I can find that connection with him. This is where we feel his love, where we allow him to enter into the painful places, the joyful places, into each and every space within us. We don't even need words of affirmation or a promise that everything will be okay. When I sit in the silence and tell God I want more of him, he fills me with a joy and a peace that solve all my problems. In this silence, we can replace our doubt with trust, and our sadness with joy.

Prayer is abandonment to God's will, which can only happen with trust. One of the best ways to have peace with God is to actually know him. We must learn to know God not as a friend but as a true lover: the one who knows everything about us, who loves us more deeply and fiercely than any other person ever will.

"Lord, you have probed me, you know me: / you know when I sit and stand" (Psalm 139:1).

# pursue holiness
*Holiness is the best gift you can give your family.*
Father Thomas Dubay, S.M. (as told to my friend Marie)

Spending time in prayer is a challenge. But let's consider what prayer is: ultimately, it's simply inviting God into every area of our heart and soul and mind and being. When we remember that, prayer is suddenly everywhere and all the time. When I recognize God's great love for me, that I am fearfully and wonderfully made, I start to love who I am. The more I love who I am, the more I trust in God's plan, his wisdom. The more I love myself, the more I love others. And all this is done through a deep connection with God.

At the heart of loving our life and wanting to be a saint comes the admission that we are imperfect people trying to grow. God loves us where we are, indeed, but we have to work to do better. In the same way the athlete doesn't want to be exactly the same a year from now, we should be open to growth, change, and moving forward on a path of sanctification.

God sees us and knows us. We can keep nothing hidden from him, and trying to run from God, or even hide the parts of ourselves we don't like, is futile.

"There is nothing which is hidden from God, but our very secrets are near to him," writes Saint Ignatius. "Let us therefore do all things as those who have him dwelling in us, that we may be his temples, and he may be in us as our God."

Embrace holiness. Embrace the desire to be a saint. As Saint Augustine recognized, "Lord, you have made us for yourself; therefore, our heart is restless until it rests in thee."

I'm always amazed by the ways God draws me closer to him by helping me deal with my issues. He loves me so much that he doesn't want me going through my life carrying the same burdens and baggage. And I'm finding that God helps us deal with things in his time.

A few years ago I went through a very painful experience. Some things I said, some ways of behaving, ended up being very hurtful to people I love a lot. I repaired the relationships, but I had to deal with the root of how I had behaved. God ended up using this experience to help me deal with the thing that caused the problem — it ended up bringing so much healing and freedom for me.

I think we've all had experiences like that. Maybe it's called "getting older" or "growing up." But I love that we will never outgrow opportunities for growth and change in our spiritual life. Not all of the experiences will be giant, heaving moments. More likely we will have lots of small, peace-filled shifts that keep drawing us forward toward Christ — aha moments, where we see bad behavior and make a connection of how to change it.

To pursue holiness is to let go of restlessness. It is unclenching a fist that clings so tightly to the things we think will bring us happiness. True adventure comes from telling God he can have his way with us.

This is simplicity at its finest. It's giving it all to God and holding on to nothing.

"God is nothing but love, straight through, and therefore the life of friendship with him, in the richest sense, is a life of total love, self-forgetting love," writes Bishop Robert Barron. "The spiritual life, at the highest pitch, is about giving your life away."

Here is the heart of adventure in Christ, of recognizing him in our hopes and dreams, and our hunger and thirst. Pursing holiness is simply recognizing that God is within every single part of who we want to be, what we want to do, in our yearning to be the best version of ourselves and do something fabulously great with our life.

Holiness is rooted in simplicity: recognizing that all the complicated strings of emotions and feelings can be redirected to God. It's remembering that we are made for God, to know him, to love him, and to serve him. This doesn't mean that we will do less with our life, but so much more. Every good thing comes from him, and he has an incredible adventure in store for each one of us, using the gifts he's given us — the beautiful, wonderful person he's created each of us to be. When we look at our journey, our pursuit of holiness, may we never be content to stay exactly where we are.

chapter 8

# spirituality and others

*There is then a two-fold movement in Faith and Sharing: an inward movement towards God hidden in the depths of our own vulnerability, and an outward movement towards our brothers and sisters, especially those who are more poor and in need.*

— Father Bill Clark, S.J.

Prayer, explains Bishop Robert Barron, is not something that we use simply to be closer to God, but rather a tool to help us share God with others.

"The point of prayer," he says, 'is not to stay on the mountain. It is not to cling to the mystical experience, however wonderful. It is to become radiant with the divine light so as to share it with the world."

So we pray, and we open ourselves to friendship with God. And then we go out into the world to love God's people. We use God's love for us to love others. And we use our interactions with others to draw us closer to God, not only in the act of sharing love but also in learning to die to ourselves. Dealing with other people can be tough. People are messy. And when we interact with the world around us, we learn to grow in so many areas (humility, patience, kindness). Jesus uses others to help us grow in holiness.

# love your spouse

*To be a saint is to be holy, and to be holy is to follow God's will, and God's will is always a will to love, and love is willing the good of the other... so to be a saint is to will the good of others.*

— Bishop Robert Barron

Marriage is super easy.

Said no married person, ever.

Honestly, though, marriage is wonderful and beautiful and good. It's also a ton of work.

Paul and I always marvel that if you embrace the whole "putting the other person's needs ahead of your own," marriage can be fun!

I like thinking about marriage through the lens of simplicity, because if you can approach loving your spouse in the most simplified, no-strings, no-attachments way, life will be amazing!

That is asking a lot. It's asking you to love extravagantly, without counting the cost. It's asking you to trust. It's asking you to forgive, move on, and let go of past grievances, and deal with hurt and then forgive again. And it's remembering that your spouse has to forgive you as well. It's humility and patience and kindness and love toward someone who has seen you at your very best and your absolute worst.

Loving your spouse is the finest opportunity for spiritual growth because it's like having a part of you (your better half) that you have to hold to the highest standard. Because your spouse is a part of you (sacramentally, spiritually), it might be tempting and easy to treat this person however you feel like treating them. Especially after a lot of time has gone by and you are comfortable with this person, it can be challenge not to let it all hang out, and not in a good way.

But a sacramental marriage means that marriage is draw-

ing us closer to God. It means this is our most important opportunity to build the Church, our part of the Church, by
working hard to love this person God has placed next to us.
Treating marriage as a part of our sanctification, as a key part
of growth in holiness — this will change the world!

Here are five ways I have found to build my marriage and
bring me peace:

1. Consider in each situation if you want to be
   right or to be happy.
2. Ask what you can do today to make your spouse
   happy. (I got this idea from Paul! He told me
   this is what he asks himself every day, and when
   I heard that I decided it was an excellent thing
   to do.)
3. Don't focus on how your spouse can be better or
   do better. We can all improve in certain areas.
   And don't compare — your friend is married
   to someone who has strengths your spouse does
   not. Oh well!
4. Pray for your spouse.
5. Pray with your spouse. Paul and I have gotten
   into the habit of taking one minute to pray with
   each other every morning before we leave the
   house. We stand and hold hands and Paul says a
   prayer for me and then I say a prayer for him. It's
   quick, simple, and powerful.
6. Work hard on your marriage. Put the other person first. If every married person wakes up each
   day and decides that this day will be all about
   making her or his spouse happy and putting his
   or her needs first, can you imagine the results?
   For you personally, in your desire to be holy. For
   the world at large. Strong marriages build the
   Church, and they strengthen our society. What
   an incredible gift to be a part of that endeavor!

# cultivate community

*I am struck by how sharing our weakness and difficulties is more
nourishing to others than sharing our qualities and successes.*
— Jean Vanier, *Community and Growth*

How many times have you felt at peace and one with nature,
Jesus, and all the saints, only to walk out your front door,
encounter somebody, and feel that grace deflate? I've had moments where I get this crazy idea that I could be a saint, if it
weren't for all the people I have to deal with!

We joke, but some days it feels true. And the minute we
feel that way, it's God gently drawing us closer to him by encouraging us to die to ourselves and grow in love and virtue.
We need to burn out a little more of ourselves and fill that
space with Jesus.

"The saints were never satisfied," said Father Jacob Al-
meter. "They were always deepening their relationship with
God."

The saints became saints by dealing with people.

It's easy to focus on the saints who lived out in the desert
and grew in holiness through pure physical suffering. I like
those saints. The rest of us find our suffering in the small acts
of mortifications — of being kind when we are tired, of being
patient when we think we have a right to be annoyed. These
are the ways we can grow in heroic virtue. God uses others to
help root out in us what must be refined. We are rocks in a
tumbler, using our encounters with one another to smooth out
the sharp edges.

In *The Love That Keeps Us Sane,* Father Marc Foley, O.C.D.,
writes about Saint Thérèse of Lisieux and her "little way" to
holiness: "The circumstances of Thérèse's life, like our own,
were ordinary," writes Father Foley. He continues:

> Every day she awoke to deal with the same people
> and same situations that she had dealt with the day
> before. However, her life was not boring because she

consciously attended to the greatest adventure of all, "penetrating into the mysterious depths of charity." Thérèse's "little way" discloses to us the inexhaustible depths of the commonplace, where each choice to love is that point of interaction of the timeless with time, where the impossible union, the mystery of the Incarnation, takes place in our lives. For it is a step-by-step journey into the heartland of the ordinary, choice upon choice, choice within choice.

The little way is the pursuit of love, and learning to love extravagantly. What does that even mean?

Distilled, to love extravagantly means loving more than we think someone deserves. It's being more patient than we think we are required to be. It's having a better view of someone than we feel he or she might deserve. It's learning to let go of our opinions and "rights" and learning to think about others more than we think about ourselves. It's not being a doormat, but it's also learning not to worry so much about whether we're being a doormat.

It's simple because there is no list to drag around, no agenda, no chart of who deserves what. It's pure freedom — and also scary as heck.

Years ago, our parish priest, Father Brett Brannen, asked one of the most profound questions I had ever heard. "Do you want to be right, or do you want to be happy?"

I asked one of my boys that same question shortly after, and he replied: "Wait, I thought being right WAS being happy?"

That's the temptation, isn't it? But learning to love others in the midst of their weakness and wounds — and thanking God for all the times you have been loved that way — brings freedom and peace and joy.

We can't love those around us unless we have experienced God's great love for us. This goes back to the importance of spending time in prayer, of spending time with the Creator.

"The soul's deepest regret," writes Father Foley, "is that it hasn't heeded its deepest vocation, the call to love."

God loves us. We learn to love others. We shed the weight of pettiness. We move about without having a plan for who deserves our love. We just love. It's simple and free.

# help your family pray

*The family that prays together, stays together.*
— Father Patrick Payton, C.S.C.

A big part of family life involves training children in the faith. This can be painful.

I'm not talking about the joy that comes from sharing Jesus with your children. If I'm living my life the way God wants me to, I shouldn't have to use too many words to tell my kids about God's love for them. If Paul and I are doing what we should, God's love for my children will be evident to them in the way we treat them and in the joy we show and offer.

BUT ...

There is the act of learning to pray too. There is the practical side of faith that involves things like family prayer, reading the Bible, learning to hear God's voice, which means getting in the habit of being quiet.

For some families, this is a real challenge. When I was starting on my journey of discovering contemplative prayer, the kind of prayer that involves experiencing God's presence in the silence and not simply through petitions and thanksgiving, I decided that introducing this concept to my five sons was important.

I brought everyone into the front room, cleared out space for everyone to kneel, and then brought a crucifix and several candles to the front of the room. I then lit the candles and proceeded to get thoroughly agitated when my boys spent the next fifteen minutes trying to blow out the candles and stick their fingers in the flame and quietly poke and jostle the brother next to them.

By the end, I was near tears (and near cussing). To which my dear, patient husband asked, "Rach. What did you expect?"

He did not ask this rhetorically. He really wanted to know, because what he saw from our boys was exactly what he expected. Flames and silence and five Balducci boys were never going to coexist.

And so, I was reminded once again that to everything there is a season. And a lot of a person's personal spiritual journey will happen, well, personally. I can set my children in the right direction and give them opportunity. But I also need to realize that God will overcome my shortcomings and limitations — including my limitations as mother of a pack of boys. He will meet our children where they are.

For now, family prayers have finally started to include the Rosary, now that the youngest is eight. And we can even go to Adoration. But I will no longer hold myself to the standard of what prayers at a friary look like. If that's God's plan for my children, he can make it happen. Our best results come from everyone being strapped in the van (no one can move!), giving everyone a chance to say what they want to pray for, and ending with a Hail Mary and a Saint Michael prayer.

What's most important in discussing family prayer (and service) is the act of learning that the world is so much bigger than our sweet little self-centered children. I say that with love.

Our job is to teach our children there is so much more to life than the next thing they want. Jesus loves them. The world is big. Let's focus on petitions (asking Jesus to help with people or things), thanksgiving (thanking God for all he has done), and acts of kindness and love to others. Have your children serve a neighbor, for free! Remind them that they are not the center of the universe. That is the heart of our job as parents. God loves them, and he has a plan for their lives. They are fearfully and wonderfully made!

All of that aside, it is important for parents to have a "pastoral plan" for each of the children. That sounds heavy, but it's simple. First off, I always try to operate with the knowledge that God loves my children more than I ever could. This takes a lot of weight off my shoulders. Paul and I will still work our very best at parenting each of our children, but it helps me operate less out of fear and more out of love.

A pastoral plan simply means that you are mindful of each individual child and what he or she is going through. You are praying with them and for them, and being aware of the ways you can help guide them in the areas they struggle with (laziness, etc.). The Holy Spirit is a powerful adviser in this. I can't tell you how many times the Holy Spirit has whispered a notion to me, perhaps to ask a certain question or check into a certain situation, only to have it help my child in an area that I honestly had no idea needed help.

Ask the Holy Spirit to guide you in your parenting. And remember to be at peace. God knew what he was doing when he gave you each of your children — and he knew what he was doing when he gave them YOU as a parent.

chapter 9

# spirituality and you

*The glory of God is man fully alive.*
— Saint Irenaeus

B eing at peace with other people requires being at peace
with yourself, within yourself, with where you are and
where you are going.

You have to have peace within before you can be okay
with the people around you. We talked about the spiritual life
and the components of Jesus (the heart of the matter) and others (where we grow a lot!). And now let's talk about ourselves.

"Spirituality and You" means spiritual self-care. It means
taking all of the other areas — the peace and order and learning to let go and simplifying — and letting them impact us in
a positive, personal way. This final section is where we overlap
the personal spiritual with the personal practical, which takes
us back to the beginning of this book and the quest for order
in a practical sense. The book ends with this topic, but really
this is where the simple life begins.

Our desire to be holy is at the heart of all of this. If holiness
didn't matter to us, we wouldn't care about positive interactions with others or strong parenting skills or real joy in the

little things. Getting the practical in order, like the menu and the laundry, helps foster the peace for the bigger things, like kindness and patience. One doesn't automatically generate the other, but each helps the other grow.

## embrace the season you are in
*Real zeal is standing still and letting God be a bonfire within you.*
— Catherine Doherty

A look at the lives of the saints reminds us that God doesn't make mistakes. Make peace with your personality, your housekeeping style, how you raise your kids, how you make a chore chart. All of those things are who you are, and when you are trying to be the best version of yourself, you have to let the rest go. Trust in God and his great, extravagant love for you.

Also, don't fight where you are at in life.

Let me tell you a story about the time my friend Rose, homeschooling mother of many, invited us over to make tilmas in honor of Juan Diego being canonized.

Rose and I both had our first four children in the same time span. The difference was that Rose had four girls and I had four boys. A few months after we each had our fourth baby (five days apart), Juan Diego was canonized a saint. In honor of his canonization, Rose invited the Balducci crew over to celebrate. It was so thoughtful of her to include us in their celebration, and she did so because Paul's mom was born and raised in Mexico City. Juan Diego and Our Lady of Guadalupe are an important part of our family heritage.

Rose's idea for the party was for each child to decorate a T-shirt to look like Juan Diego's tilma — a beautiful image of Our Lady, and flowers on the bottom to represent what appeared when Juan Diego opened it.

Except, the Balducci boys had no interest in drawing a lady on a T-shirt. Swords, dinosaurs, Legos — those would all be acceptable. But a lady? No way.

It didn't matter that it was Our Lady and that she was the Queen of the Universe. And no amount of me begging and pleading and quietly threatening convinced them to do what Rose had invited us for. What kind of a good, Catholic mother am I that I can't get my young sons to paint a picture of Mary of the front of their T-shirts?

So much time has gone by now that what amazes me most is not that they wouldn't cooperate but how personally I took it. Now I know better. At the time, I took it as a personal failure that my young sons — aged two, three, and five — had no interest in drawing Our Lady on their shirts. They knew what they liked, and that wasn't it. I saw this as a failure in my ability as a Catholic mother to instill a deep and abiding love of Mary our Mother.

Meanwhile, Rose's girls were simply giddy at the opportunity. Their love for Our Lady and the joy of painting her image on a T-shirt was thrilling. I spent those few hours feeling dejected and lame.

This story stands out for me because it was hilarious. I allowed the whole scene of eight children under the age of five working on T-shirts to be a reflection (in my mind) of my abilities as a mother and a lover of Christ. In the midst of that, I had a stark awakening in my role as a mother of boys. I realized, once we were home and I had gotten so mad at my little boys, that I couldn't force them to be who I wanted them to be. God had given me a brood of boys, and my job as their mom was going to look a lot different than Rose's job of raising her girls. We each had a totally unique call and a beautiful opportunity as mothers.

That experience helped me learn to love my job as a mom to boys. It also helped me begin to love myself.

In recognizing how different I was going to be as a mother, I recognized my responsibility to be myself. I couldn't try to parent like Rose because I didn't have her children — and I wasn't her!

A tremendous weight was lifted when I stopped trying to

be someone else. I had to make an act of courage. I had to learn not to be defeated as a mother, as a human being.

"Humility," says Father Jacques Philippe, "is consenting to our inner poverty."

My seven-year-old daughter, Isabel, was working on a writing project for school. She was struggling, getting agitated, and wishing it was over. "I'm not good at this. I don't like writing!" She said it a few times and then stopped. "If I say discouraging things to myself," she noted, "then I don't do as well."

Isn't that the truth! We seem to function in the manner that we expect we will. When we think things are difficult or we focus on how much we don't like doing a certain task, the struggle is real. And so it goes with how we think about ourselves. If all we think about are the ways we could be better, how we can change things about ourselves, or the parts of us we don't like, we become a product of that kind of thinking.

This mentality is particularly prevalent for those pursuing life in Christ. When we strive to "be better," we risk seeing ourselves as something broken, in need of repair. Of course, we are broken, in need of repair, but our redemption comes from God alone, not our own ability to fix ourselves.

I spent years wanting to be a better version of myself (I still do, of course), but in the midst of that I got confused about what that meant.

Be who you are, who God made you to be. Love where you are, trust that where you're at is where God wants you to be. Learn from this moment, asking God to show you how.

You can tweak areas and work to improve, but you can't let a focus on holiness get confused with self-loathing. True holiness, growing deeper in love with Jesus, will actually yield more love of self, because you will become more aware of God's great love for you.

A huge part of this will be acknowledging the season of life you are in. You are moving and growing as a human, and your season is a big part of that. Life with small children will absolutely impact where you can go and what you can do. Life with teenagers will do the same. The beautiful thing is how God uses each season to do something powerful within us. It's that Duty of the Moment, and I love how God has a plan for each one of us based on who we are and what we are going through. There is a purpose for all of it.

Once upon a time, I was getting so frustrated with two of my small children, and how impossible they were to put to bed at night, that I started pretending I worked in a nursing home: they were an old man named Howard and an old lady named Myrtle. Suddenly, instead of wishing I could get them to go to sleep already, I saw these moments as a task of real importance. In the way I would have cared for two elderly people I was getting paid to care for, I gave my kids that level of my energy. "Now which one of you wanted one last drink of water before bed," I asked, with all the patience in the world. And they loved it. They pretended to be old people, and we had some fun.

That's weird, but here's my point: I was getting so bogged down in trying to move through this painful event (bedtime can be painful) that I was losing track of this time and place and its importance in my life. I don't always act like that, but in moments of real desperation I try to get outside my head and see the bigger picture. It helps.

Embrace the season you are in. Maybe it's a great season. Maybe you feel like you are going crazy. Give it back to God, ask for grace and wisdom, and remember that he's using it all to draw you closer to him.

# get out of that funk
*Sometimes you're the windshield; sometimes you're the bug.*
— Mark Knopfler

Remember that story I told you about going for my annual exam and freaking out on my doctor? Well, I left that visit with a prescription for Xanax.

I wasn't sure how I felt about that. It caught me off guard, frankly. I'm not opposed to meds, but I didn't go into that appointment thinking I needed any. I stared at that slip of paper for days. I put it in my top drawer and would look at it each time I opened the drawer. Some days I picked up that scrip and thought about what it meant that my doctor gave that to me after listening to me. I talked and he listened, and he heard a woman on complete overload.

And I didn't even realize.

That appointment was weeks before this whole story began, before I realized I was on overload and feeling sad, tired, and worn out. I thought I was handling everything fine — no big deal that my blood pressure was skyrocketing because I'm so scared to be at the doctor.

But my doctor heard me, and he knew I needed help. It was time for some very personal, spiritual peace and order.

Now, this kind of discussion always gets a little tricky because taking care of the very core of ourselves requires countless delicate maneuvers. Your interior life is like a sound mixing board, with so many different knobs, buttons, and faders that work together to make you whole. Ultimately, Jesus is at the center of it, but it's dangerous folly to sit back and passively say, "Jesus loves me and will take care of me." That is absolutely true, but God gave us a brain, and we need to use it.

That means we become aware of all the different knobs and buttons, what each of them is and means, and how they operate separately and together. And we consider how each component is doing. We take the practical, the personal, and the spiritual — and all the ways they interact with one another — and go from there.

If your home life is out of order, you will suffer.

If your emotional and mental life is out of order, you will suffer.

If your spiritual life is out of order, you will suffer.

And if you are in a season where the realities and obligations of life prevent any one of these from operating at an ideal level, we thank God for the gift of modern medicine. Because when our chemical levels are off, or our serotonin is depleted, or life has handed us something that needs more than a better prayer time, we have to be willing to accept the help we need.

If you have ever been in this position, dealing with the anxiety and fear caused by extreme stress, hormone imbalance, or depression, you know the beauty of seeking help and getting it. It is life-changing.

What's beneficial about a simple life is that when something is out of order, you can assess it. When you have identified the disorder and adjusted things, you will have peace. And when you've identified the disorder but are not in a position to change or adjust, you can do something about that as well.

Being at peace with yourself means knowing you are loved by God, being aware of the many moving parts of your life, and working to keep them streamlined. You address stressors and see what you can do about them.

Sometimes a funk is only a few hard days. Offer it up, push through. Hormones are mean, my friend. It's gonna be okay.

Sometimes a funk goes on a little longer. Offer it up, push through, keep track of how long it's been. Pinpoint the problem and see what can be done.

In those weeks of staring at that prescription slip in my drawer, I found that I needed to have an honest conversation. I needed to talk with myself and with my husband about my stress levels. The solution ended up involving some major life changes, which brought me the emotional peace and order I needed. This wasn't simply to avoid taking medication, but it ended up relieving the need to. My family needed me more than the job did, and stepping back took off the incredible stress that was creating the problem in the first place.

If you find yourself in a stressful season, don't keep it to yourself. Be honest with someone around you. Personal spiritual self-care might include going on a retreat or talking to a therapist. It might be as simple as outsourcing childcare so you can catch your breath, or outsourcing cleaning so you can relax with your family.

And it might involve medication, for a season or indefinitely. Be open to that as a solution. We live in a world that moves at a pace far faster than our bodies were designed to operate. We can find as many ways to adjust as possible, but it's important to remember that medicine is a viable, effective option.

## don't be a martyr, be yourself!

*No matter how much you think you are searching for God,*
*he is searching for you more.*
— Saint John of the Cross

Simplicity of self. Is that a thing? In the times that I feel the most free and the closest to God, I recognize a lightness that is either through grace or perseverance. Maybe a bit of both.

We carry so many burdens with us, things we latch on to and keep in our grasp. What are these things? Why are they so important? Ideals, opinions, our own little view of the world crafted from our experience, from wounds and fears, and also victory and hard-wrought dedication. We are a mixture of all of these things, and if we aren't careful, they can become quite a burden.

*With Open Hands* is Henri Nouwen's simple and profound book on personal prayer. In it, he describes prayer as a relationship in which "you allow the other to enter into the very center of your person, allow him to speak there, allow him to touch the sensitive core of your being, and allow him to see so much that you would rather leave in darkness."

Nouwen talks about a resistance to praying that involves an inability to let go:

> The resistance to pray is like the resistance of tightly clenched fists. This image shows the tension, the desire to cling tightly to yourself, a greediness which betrays fear. The story about an old woman brought to a psy-

chiatric center exemplifies this attitude. She was wild, swinging at everything in sight, and scaring everyone so much that the doctors had to take everything away from her. But there was one small coin which she gripped in her fist and would not give up. In fact, it took two men to pry open that squeezed hand. It was as though she would lose her very self along with the coin. If they deprived her of that last possession, she would have nothing more, and be nothing more. That was her fear.

And so it is with prayer. We are that old woman. When we enter into prayer, into a relationship with the Creator, we are asked to let go of all that we cling to so very tightly.

"But who wants to do that?" writes Nouwen. "A first prayer, therefore, is often a painful prayer, because you discover you don't want to let go. You hold fast to what is familiar, even if you aren't proud of it. You find yourself saying: 'That's just how it is with me. I would like it to be different, but it can't be now. That's the way it is, and that's the way I'll have to leave it.'... You feel safer to cling to a sorry past than to trust in a new future. So you fill your hands with small clammy coins which you don't want to surrender."

We hold on to so many things. We cling to past hurts and past images of ourselves. We hold on to our attitudes and opinions. Before long, you've got a backpack of conceptions and misconceptions that you carry everywhere you go. It's heavy and cumbersome, but somehow we think it keeps us safe.

"Detachment," says Nouwen, "is often understood as letting loose of what is attractive. But it can also mean being attached to what is repulsive. You can become attached to your own hate.... When you dare to let go and surrender one of those many fears, your hand relaxes and your palms spread out in a gesture of receiving. You must have patience, of course, before your hands are completely open and their muscles relaxed."

The challenge is not only to forgive yourself for all the ways you've sinned, but to finally let go of your ideas, your hurts — to open your hands and give those things to God. Nouwen writes:

> What is possible is to open your hands without fear, so the other can blow your sins away. For perhaps it isn't clammy coins, but just a light dust which a soft breeze will whirl away, leaving only a grin or a chuckle behind. Then you feel a bit of new freedom, and praying becomes a joy, a spontaneous reaction to the world and the people around you. Praying becomes effortless, inspired and lively, or peaceful and quiet. Then you recognize the festive and the modest as moments of prayer. You begin to suspect that to pray is to live.

That emptiness, that letting go, is God's opportunity to enter and fill us with himself.

"God cannot fill what is full," said Mother Teresa. "He can fill only emptiness — deep poverty — and your 'yes' [to Jesus] is the beginning of being or becoming empty. It is not how much we 'have' to give — but how empty we are — so that we can receive fully in our life and let him live his life in us. In you today — he wants to relive his complete submission to his father — allow him to do so.... Take away your eyes from yourself and rejoice that you have nothing."

All the things in our life — our spouse, our kids, the people we love — are gifts from God. But they cannot be what brings us peace and joy and fulfillment. That must be the space that we are willing to pour out so that God may fill it with himself. In that fullness, we find true peace and true happiness.

Hope is the confident expectation of a coming good. If our hope is rooted in our kids or our present situation, then life is going to be very hard. You can't put your joy on hold while your kids get through a difficult season. Our well-being can't be a lack of difficulty.

All these things were said to me by my friend and spiritual director Bev. She was talking me down off some crazy in a season where I realized I was walking around with my fists balled up very tightly (figuratively speaking) as I waited for one of my children to start making better decisions. I told Paul on our walk the day before that my life felt a little on hold. I was waiting for my kids to all be settled and secure, and then I could go back to being free and joyous.

That's not healthy. Our joy and peace come from the Lord, not from our circumstances. We work to find peace and order, and then we hand all of that over to Jesus.

What does this have to do with being a martyr? It's the letting go. It's not trying so hard to be perfect. It's pursuing due diligence in all the areas of our life and trusting God to take care of the rest. It's not taking ourselves so seriously that when we mess up we feel like a failure.

The most humble thing we can do is accept our weakness and love ourselves in our own imperfections.

"That is real humility," writes Father Jacques Philippe in *The Way of Trust and Love*, "to accept ourselves as we are, to love ourselves as we are. And it attracts God's grace very powerfully."

# conclusion

*The fruit of silence is prayer,*
*The fruit of prayer is faith,*
*The fruit of faith is love,*
*The fruit of love is service,*
*The fruit of service is peace.*

— Saint Teresa of Calcutta

Make my life simple in thirty-some easy steps. Maybe it doesn't seem so simple. But it is!

A simple life filled with order and peace means giving each part of our busy, beautiful, abundant life the attention it deserves.

It means taking time for the little things so they don't become big things.

When the little things are in order, we can focus on the big things, the things that should take our attention. The simple life means acknowledging all the different aspects and ignoring none of them, and dealing with things in good order so we don't feel compelled to ignore them.

Each one of us will have different solutions to the different areas of life. Life is grand that way! My friend Colleen realized a few years ago that her babies were getting bigger, and she was ready for a new challenge. My friend Susie and I suggested maybe training for a 5K or redecorating her front room. Colleen decided to quit her job and open a pie shop. Variety is the spice of life!

We will each have areas that we find more worthy of our time and effort. I can promise you that if I have to choose between cleaning the house or preparing an elaborate meal for dinner, the house will be scrubbed, and we will be eating quesadillas. That's how I roll.

And you get to roll your way. Be inspired by your friends and their gifts, and then do what works best for you. Find peace and order in all the small ways of doing business, because those add up to the big business of freedom and joy.

Keeping your bathroom clean can make you a saint. It's weird, and it's true. All of these things, the moving parts of the abundant life, are meant to bring us closer to Jesus. Caring for my home, my domestic church, is the thing God is asking of me now. So I clean and cook and organize and streamline. I focus on my health and my relationships, on my prayer life and my mental well-being.

These are all the parts of me, my life, my journey toward being a saint. Every single part of what I have going on, being a mom, a wife, a daughter, a friend: these are all my opportunities to grow and love and die to myself.

God is with us in the journey and in the fruit. He's there in our victories and our failures. We fall, we get up, we dust ourselves off, and we adjust. We keep moving forward, grateful for the gift of life and the journey of learning to hear God's voice in the midst of it all.